**A Clean Break, Royal Court Theatre and
Royal Exchange Theatre co-production**

WITHDRAWN

11 JUN 2023

by Vivienne Franzmann

First performed at Royal Exchange Theatre, Manchester,
on 12 March 2014

Pests is part of the Royal Court Theatre's Playwrights programme,
supported by the Foundation

by Vivienne Franzmann

CAST

ROLLY **Ellie Kendrick**
PINK **Sinéad Matthews**

CREATIVE TEAM

DIRECTOR **Lucy Morrison**
DESIGNER **Joanna Scotcher**
LIGHTING DESIGNER **Fabiana Piccioli**
SOUND DESIGNER **Emma Laxton**
VIDEO DESIGNER **Kim Beveridge**

12–22 March 2014
Royal Exchange Theatre, Manchester
Box Office 0161 833 9833
www.royalexchange.co.uk

27 March–3 May 2014
Jerwood Theatre Upstairs, Royal Court Theatre, London
Box Office 020 7565 5000
www.royalcourttheatre.com

22–24 May 2014
Traverse Theatre, Edinburgh
Box Office 0131 228 1404
www.traversetheatre.co.uk

28–31 May 2014
Studio, Everyman Playhouse, Liverpool
Box Office 0151 709 4776
www.everymanplayhouse.com

3–7 June 2014
The Drum, Plymouth Theatre Royal, Plymouth
Box Office 0175 226 7222
www.theatreroyal.com

11–14 June 2014
Birmingham Repertory Theatre, Birmingham
Box Office 0121 236 4455
www.birmingham-rep.co.uk

Cast and Creative Team

Vivienne Franzmann (Writer)
Vivienne Franzmann was a teacher for thirteen years in a variety of London secondary schools. In 2008, she was one of four winners of the Bruntwood Playwriting Award with her first play *Mogadishu* and went on to be awarded the George Devine Award for Most Promising Playwright in 2010. *Mogadishu* was performed at the Manchester Royal Exchange and at the Lyric Theatre in Hammersmith in 2011. Her second play, *The Witness* won her a Pearson Playwrights' Bursary and an attachment to the Royal Court. *The Witness* premiered at the Royal Court in 2012. Vivienne was Resident Playwright for Clean Break in 2012 and has taught the playwriting course several times. She has written for Channel 4, BBC 1, Radio 4 and Radio 3. She is currently under commission to the Almeida Theatre, the Royal Court and Washington Studios.

Lucy Morrison (Director)
Lucy is Head of Artistic Programme for Clean Break. For the company she has directed and developed *Billy the Girl* by Katie Hims (Soho Theatre); *Little on the inside* by Alice Birch (Almeida Festival, Latitude 2013); *it felt empty when the heart went at first but it is alright now* by Lucy Kirkwood (Arcola Theatre); *This Wide Night* by Chloë Moss (Soho Theatre/Theatre Live, Newcastle/ Drum Theatre, Plymouth). Lucy originated and commissioned the *Charged* and *Re-Charged* seasons (Soho Theatre) in which she directed *Fatal Light* by Chloë Moss and *Doris Day* by EV Crowe. Alongside heading up Clean Break's Artistic Programme, Lucy was Artistic Director of the Almeida Festival 2013. She was formerly Literary Manager of Paines Plough, where she worked with many of the country's most exciting playwrights including Dennis Kelly, Abi Morgan, Sarah Kane, Mark Ravenhill and Jack Thorne. Other directing credits include *Housekeeping* (Southwark Playhouse/ Latitude Festival 2011) and *Product* (Traverse Theatre/Royal Court Theatre Upstairs/European tour).

Joanna Scotcher (Designer)
Joanna received the Whatsonstage 'Best Set Designer' Award for her site-specific design of *The Railway Children*, which went on to win the Olivier Award for Best Entertainment in 2011. Joanna was trained at the Royal Shakespeare Company. From this classical initiation in stage design, her design projects have taken her from performances on lakes, through journeys under forgotten London, to games in Royal Palaces. As well as her theatrical stage design, her work specialises in the world of immersive performance and site-responsive design, inhabiting spaces from the epic to the intimate. Her recent design work has been exhibited at the V&A Museum's *From Gaga to Gormley* exhibition, while her immersive series of installations *House of Cards* can currently be seen at Kensington Palace. Joanna forms part of the award-winning theatre company LookLeftLookRight as associate designer. To view her portfolio please visit: www.joannascotcher.com

Fabiana Piccioli (Lighting Designer)
Fabiana studied Philosophy at University La Sapienza di Roma.
From 1999 to 2002 she worked as a dancer in Rome and Brussels.
She then became Technical Coordinator and Production Manager at
the Romaeuropa Festival in 2002–2004 before joining Akram Khan
Company as Technical Manager in 2005. She was Lighting Designer
for three of the company's productions: *Variations for Vibes, Strings
and Pianos*, and *bahok*; as well as *Gnosis* for the *Svapnagata
Festival*, curated by Nitin Sawhney and Akram Khan at Sadler's
Wells. She also co-designed the set for *bahok*.

Emma Laxton (Sound Designer)
Emma has worked extensively at the Royal Court, where she was
Deputy Head of Sound, and was previously an Associate Artist at the
Bush Theatre. Her theatre credits include: for the Royal Court: *The
Westbridge, The Heretic, Tusk Tusk, Faces in the Crowd, That Face*
(and West End), *Gone Too Far!, My Name is Rachel Corrie* (West
End, New York and Edinburgh Festival); *Bone, Bear Hug, Terrorism,
Food Chain, The Blackest Black, #AIWW: The Arrest of Ai Wei Wei,
Lay Down Your Cross, Blue Heart Afternoon* (Hampstead Theatre);
*Coriolanus, Berenice, The Physicists, Making Noise Quietly, The
Recruiting Officer* (Donmar Warehouse); *All My Sons, A Doll's
House, Three Birds, The Accrington Pals, Lady Windermere's Fan*
(Royal Exchange); *There Are Mountains* (Clean Break, HMP Askham
Grange); *Charged* (Clean Break, Soho Theatre); *Men Should Weep*
(National Theatre); *Black T-Shirt Collection* (Fuel UK tour and
National Theatre); *Where's My Seat, Like A Fishbone, The Whiskey
Taster, If There Is I Haven't Found It Yet; 2nd May 1997, Apologia,
The Contingency Plan, Wrecks, Broken Space Season, 2000 Feet
Away* (Bush Theatre); and many more.

Kim Beveridge (Video Designer)
Since graduating from Duncan of Jordanstone College of Art and
Design in 2005 with a BA Honours degree in 'Time Based Art', Kim
has been working as a freelance digital artist, documentary film
maker, video designer for live performance and sound artist. She is
an associate artist with Tricky Hat Productions and work to date
includes *Whatever Gets You Through The Night* for the Arches,
winner of Creative Scotland Best Theatre Award 2013; *The Missing
Audio Journey,* a site-specific art installation for the National Theatre
of Scotland at Tramway; *Roadkill,* a multi award-winning site-specific
piece of theatre for Pachamama Productions; and *Wall of Death*, a
collaboration with National Theatre of Scotland's Stephen Skrynka,
documenting his quest to learn to ride the Wall of Death with the
world-famous Ken Fox Troupe. www.kimbeveridge.co.uk

Ellie Kendrick (Rolly)
Ellie's theatre credits include *The Low Road* and *In the Republic of Happiness* at the Royal Court, and *Romeo and Juliet* at Shakespeare's Globe. Film credits include *Cheerful Weather for the Wedding* and *An Education*. Ellie's television credits include *Game of Thrones*; *Misfits*; *Chickens*; *Being Human*; *Upstairs Downstairs* and the title role in the BBC's most recent adaptation of *The Diary of Anne Frank*.

Sinéad Matthews (Pink)
Sinéad's recent theatre credits include *Blurred Lines* (National Theatre); *Trout Stanley* (Southwark Playhouse); *The Master and Margarita* (Barbican) and she last appeared at the Royal Court in *A Time to Reap*. Sinéad's television credits include the Sky 1 drama *The Smoke, Way to Go* for BBC 3 and *Black Mirror – Be Right Back* for Channel 4. Her film credits include *Untitled Mike Leigh 2013*; *Wreckers; Nanny McPhee and The Big Bang; The Boat That Rocked; Pride and Prejudice* and *Vera Drake*.

Ali Beale (Production Manager)
Ali has worked in theatre, opera, film, dance, performance and installation, including both national and international tours. She is also Production Manager and Co-Designer for Fevered Sleep. Recent work includes *Billy the Girl*, *Re-Charged*, *Just Act*, *it felt empty…*, *Missing Out*, *This Wide Night* and *Black Crows* (Clean Break); *Above Me The Wide Blue Sky*, *Little Universe*, *It's the Skin You're Living In*, *Still Life with Dog*, *The Weather Factory*, *On Ageing*, *The Bounce*, *The Forest*, *Brilliant*, *Stilled*, *An Infinite Line Brighton*, *And the Rain Falls Down*, *The Summer Subversive*, *Fleet*, *The Field of Miracles* and *Feast Your Eyes* (Fevered Sleep); *The Contents of a House* and *Guided Tour* (Peter Reder touring to Gijon, Pittsburgh, Arizona, Singapore, Bucharest and Moscow); *Kingdom of Earth* (Three-Legged Theatre); *The Kingdom* (The Print Room); *Under Glass*, *Must*, *Performing Medicine*, *Sampled* and *Fantastic Voyage* (The Clod Ensemble); *The Evocation of Papa Mas*, *The Firework Maker's Daughter*, *Aladdin*, *Playing the Victim*, *A Little Fantasy* and *Shoot Me in The Heart* (Told by An Idiot); *Gumbo Jumbo* (The Gogmagogs); *The Ratcatcher of Hamlin* (Cartoon De Salvo); *Oogly Boogly* (Tom Morris and Guy Dartnel); *Throat* (Company FZ); *Arcane* (Opera Circus).

Beth Hoare-Barnes (Company Stage Manager)
Beth is a freelancer, who in the last year has toured to Taipei with *Brilliant* (Fevered Sleep) and CSM'd a fully staged opera on a Suffolk beach, *Peter Grimes* (Aldeburgh Music), both of which have been made into films. Diverse other projects include *Dogs Don't Do Ballet* (Little Angel); *Doonreagan* (CTCo); *Above Me The Wide Blue Sky* (Fevered Sleep/Young Vic); *The Kingdom* by Colin Teevan (Soho Theatre); the operas of *Where The Wild Things Are* and *Higglety Pigglety Pop!* (Aldeburgh Music); *The Forest* (Fevered Sleep, national tour and Sydney Opera House); and *Reykjavik* (Shams Theatre), an immersive piece at the Roundhouse. Beth has also worked with Akademi South Asian Dance, Shakespeare's Globe, Regent's Park, Unicorn Theatre and Theatre-Rites, among others. Previously she spent four years in the US studying and working as a stage manager and lighting designer, where she received an MFA and designed professionally in New York, Cleveland and Columbus.

Becky Smith (Technical Stage Manager)
Becky works as a theatre stage manager and sound designer. Previous shows with Clean Break include *Billy the Girl, it felt empty…, Missing Out, A Just Act* and *This Wide Night.* She has worked with companies including Fingersmiths, Root Theatre, Hull Truck, ATC, Risking Enchantment, Goat and Monkey, The Gate, Sherman Theatre, Polka Theatre and Oily Cart.

Emily Walker (Technical Trainee)
Emily is currently a Technical Trainee at the Royal Court. For them she has worked as a Lighting Trainee on *Brand New Ancients* by Kate Tempest (JTD); *Let The Right One In*, a stage adaption by Jack Thorne (JTD); *Gastronauts*, created by April de Angelis, Nessah Muthy and Wils Wilson (JTU); and as a stage trainee on *Not I, Footfalls, Rockaby* by Samuel Beckett (JTD), *The Mistress Contract* by Abi Morgan (JTD) and *The Pass* by John Donnelly (JTU). Emily also worked as a technical assistant on the school tour of *Pigeons* by Suhayla El-Bushra.

For *Pests*

Production Team
Senior Producer **Helen Pringle**
Head of Engagement **Imogen Ashby**
Producer **Ros Terry**
Production Manager **Ali Beale**
Company Stage Manager **Beth Hoare-Barnes**
Technical Stage Manager **Becky Smith**
Technical Trainee **Emily Walker**
Casting Director **Lotte Hines**
Movement Director **Imogen Knight**
Voice Coach **Louise Jones**
Assistant to the Lighting Designer **Sander Loonen**
Production Manager, Royal Court **Niall Black**
Production Manager, Royal Exchange **Keith Broom**
Set, Costumes and Technical support provided by
Royal Exchange Production Departments
Clean Break Stageworks placement **Samantha White**

Clean Break Marketing and Press Team
General Manager **Molly McPhee**
Marketing Assistant **Caroline Boss**
Marketing Consultants **The Cogency**
Press Consultant **Nancy Poole PR**

Clean Break Executive Director
Lucy Perman MBE

Thanks

The thanks of the cast, crew and company go to the staff and women
of HMP Styal, HMP Holloway, HMP Askham Grange, HMP Low Newton
and Arnold Lodge Medium Secure Unit, Suzanne Bell, Christine
Entwisle, Nick Malbon, the staff and students of York St John University,
Marilyn Galvin, Julia Horan, Verity La Roche, Sonya Hale, Lorna Brown,
David McSeveney, Claire Wardroper, Impact, Zamo, Daniel Simpson,
Jonathan McGuiness, Keith Chanter, Ashley Tilbury, Amber Priestley
Karina Garnett, Frances Adams.

CLEAN BREAK

Acclaimed theatre company Clean Break produces ground-breaking
plays with women writers and actors at the heart of its work.
Founded in 1979 by two women prisoners who needed urgently to
tell their stories through theatre, the company today has an
independent education programme delivering theatre opportunities to
women offenders and women at risk, in custodial and community
settings. Clean Break's innovative education work combined with
visionary expertise in theatre makes for a powerful mix. Celebrated
by critics and audiences across the UK, the company's award-
winning plays hit a collective nerve, humanising some of the most
difficult things we need to talk about as a society.

Recent productions include Katie Hims' *Billy the Girl* (Soho Theatre);
Roz Wyllie's *Stepping Off the Edge of the World* (Soho Theatre and
touring); Alice Birch's *Little on the inside* (Almeida and Latitude);
Rebecca Prichard's *Dream Pill* (Almeida, Edinburgh Fringe 2011 and
touring); Sonya Hale's *Hours til Midnight* (Latitude, Southbank Centre
and touring); *There Are Mountains* by Chloë Moss (HMP & YOI
Askham Grange); *Re-Charged*, three plays by Sam Holcroft, Rebecca
Lenkiewicz, Chloë Moss (Soho Theatre London 2011); *Charged*, a
season of six plays by E V Crowe, Sam Holcroft, Rebecca
Lenkiewicz, Chloë Moss, Winsome Pinnock & Rebecca Prichard
(Soho Theatre London 2010); *it felt empty when the heart went at first
but it is alright now* by Lucy Kirkwood (Arcola Theatre London 2009,
joint winner of the John Whiting Award 2010); and *This Wide Night* by
Chloë Moss (Soho Theatre London 2008 and revived in 2009, winner
of the Susan Smith Blackburn Award 2009). Writers currently under
commission include Sonya Hale, Roz Wyllie, Morgan Lloyd Malcolm,
Zawe Ashton, Rachel De-lahay, Stacey Gregg, Alice Birch.

Make a donation and make a difference to more women's lives

Clean Break aims to bring about change directly in the lives of the women we work with and at a national level, by changing attitudes to women and crime through theatre, education and new writing. Clean Break helps women break the cycle of crime, give voice to their experiences, and move towards positive futures.

Demand for our services is high, and our work is only possible thanks to the support of our donors. Every donation, large or small, makes a difference, and for every £1.00 invested in Clean Break £4.57 is saved to the public purse through reduced offending. What's more, we can currently double the value of your support thanks to match funding from Arts Council England's Catalyst Arts programme.

We have ambitious plans for:

- more education work, affecting the lives of individual women and supporting them through their time at Clean Break onto further or higher education, employment or voluntary work
- new writing projects for professional and non-professional women writers
- increased work with young women offenders and those at risk of offending
- increased touring to theatres and prisons with accompanying education work
- supported writing programmes for women in prison
- training for artists and criminal justice professionals wanting to learn more about our ways of working.

Clean Break is a registered charity, and our work is possible thanks to support from individuals and organisations who share our commitment to transforming the lives of vulnerable women affected by the criminal justice system. If you would like to find out more about supporting Clean Break, please contact: Sue Canderton, Head of Development, on 020 7482 8608 or **sue.canderton@cleanbreak.org.uk.**

You can also text '**CBTC14**' followed by your chosen amount (for example, to donate £10 text '**CBTC14 £10**') to **70070** to support Clean Break and make a difference today, or you can donate directly online via our website at www.cleanbreak.org.uk. Thank you.

For Clean Break

Executive Director **Lucy Perman MBE**
Head of Finance and Senior Producer **Helen Pringle**
Head of Artistic Programme **Lucy Morrison**
Head of Education **Anna Herrmann**
Head of Engagement **Imogen Ashby**
Head of Development **Sue Canderton**
Assistant Head of Education (Learning) **Vishni Velada-Billson**
Assistant Head of Education (Student Services) **Jacqueline Stewart**
General Manager **Molly McPhee**
Producer **Ros Terry**
Theatre Education Manager **Lorraine Faissal**
Theatre Education Manager **Laura McCluskey**
Development Manager **Lillian Ashford**
Student Support Worker **Ella Mountjoy**
Locum Student Support Worker **Amete Hewitt**
Outreach Worker **Lauren Sammé**
Finance Administrator **Won Fyfe**
Executive Assistant **Nicole Elizabeth**
Education Assistant **Verity La Roche**
Marketing Assistant **Caroline Boss**
Cleaner **Pauline Bernard**

Board of Directors
Kim Evans OBE (Chair), Suzanne Bell, Jude Boyles, Deborah Coles, Doreen Foster, Lucy Kirkwood, Alice Millest, Sonali Naik, Kate Paradine, Susan J Royce, Despina Tsatsas, Denise White

Patrons
Lord Paul Boateng, Carmen Callil, Dame Judi Dench DBE, Sir Richard Eyre CBE, Barbara Hosking CBE, Baroness Helena Kennedy QC, Ann Mitchell, Yve Newbold LLB, Baroness Usha Prashar CBE, Dr Joan Scanlon JP, Baroness Vivien Stern CBE, Dame Janet Suzman DBE, Emma Thompson, Dame Harriet Walter DBE, Lia Williams

Clean Break
2 Patshull Road
London
NW5 2LB
Registered company number 2690758
Registered charity number 1017560

Tel: 020 7482 8600
Fax: 020 7482 8611
general@cleanbreak.org.uk
www.cleanbreak.org.uk
facebook.com/cleanbreak
@CleanBrk

Supported using public funding by
ARTS COUNCIL ENGLAND

LOTTERY FUNDED

Clean Break would like to acknowledge the generous support of all its funders and supporters. Clean Break is a member of ITC.

JERWOOD CHARITABLE FOUNDATION

Jerwood New Playwrights is a longstanding partnership between the Jerwood Charitable Foundation and the Royal Court. 2014 is the 20th anniversary of the programme which supports the production of three new works by emerging writers, all of whom are in the first 10 years of their career.

The Royal Court carefully identifies playwrights whose careers would benefit from the challenge and profile of being fully produced either in the Jerwood Downstairs or Jerwood Upstairs Theatres at the Royal Court.

Since 1994, the programme has produced a collection of challenging and outspoken works which explore a variety of new forms and voices and so far has supported the production of 79 new plays. These plays include: Nick Payne's CONSTELLATIONS, Vivienne Franzmann's THE WITNESS, E.V. Crowe's HERO, Anya Reiss' SPUR OF THE MOMENT and THE ACID TEST, Penelope Skinner's THE VILLAGE BIKE, Rachel De-lahay's THE WESTBRIDGE, Joe Penhall's SOME VOICES, Mark Ravenhill's SHOPPING AND FUCKING (co-production with Out of Joint), Ayub Khan Din's EAST IS EAST (co-production with Tamasha), Martin McDonagh's THE BEAUTY QUEEN OF LEENANE (co-production with Druid Theatre Company), Conor McPherson's THE WEIR, Nick Grosso's REAL CLASSY AFFAIR, Sarah Kane's 4.48 PSYCHOSIS, Gary Mitchell's THE FORCE OF CHANGE, David Eldridge's UNDER THE BLUE SKY, David Harrower's PRESENCE, Simon Stephens' HERONS, Roy Williams' CLUBLAND, Leo Butler's RE-DUNDANT, Michael Wynne's THE PEOPLE ARE FRIENDLY, David Greig's OUTLYING IS-LANDS, Zinnie Harris' NIGHTINGALE AND CHASE, Grae Cleugh's FUCKING GAMES, Rona Munro's IRON, Richard Bean's UNDER THE WHALEBACK, Ché Walker's FLESH WOUND, Roy Williams' FALLOUT, Mick Mahoney's FOOD CHAIN, Ayub Khan Din's NOTES ON FALLING LEAVES, Leo Butler's LUCKY DOG, Simon Stephens' COUNTRY MUSIC, Laura Wade's BREATHING CORPSES, debbie tucker green's STONING MARY, David Eldridge's INCOMPLETE AND RANDOM ACTS OF KINDNESS, Gregory Burke's ON TOUR, Stella Feehily's O GO MY MAN, Simon Stephens' MOTORTOWN, Simon Farquhar's RAINBOW KISS, April de Angelis, Stella Feehily, Tanika Gupta, Chloe Moss and Laura Wade's CATCH, Mike Bartlett's MY CHILD, Polly Stenham's THAT FACE, Alexi Kaye Campbell's THE PRIDE, Fiona Evans' SCARBOROUGH, Levi David Addai's OXFORD STREET, Bola Agbaje's GONE TOO FAR!, Alia Bano's SHADES, Polly Stenham's TUSK TUSK, Tim Crouch's THE AUTHOR, Bola Agbaje's OFF THE ENDZ and DC Moore's THE EMPIRE.

In 2013, Jerwood New Playwrights supported Rachel De-lahay's ROUTES, Anders Lustgarten's IF YOU DON'T LET US DREAM, WE WON'T LET YOU SLEEP, Suhayla El-Bushra's PIGEONS, Clare Lizzimore's MINT and Alistair McDowall's TALK SHOW.

The Jerwood Charitable Foundation is dedicated to imaginative and responsible revenue funding of the arts, supporting artists to develop and grow at important stages in their careers. It works with artists across art forms, from dance and theatre to literature, music and the visual arts.

www.jerwoodcharitablefoundation.org.

THE ENGLISH STAGE COMPANY AT THE ROYAL COURT THEATRE

'For me the theatre is really a religion or way of life. You must decide what you feel the world is about and what you want to say about it, so that everything in the theatre you work in is saying the same thing ... A theatre must have a recognisable attitude. It will have one, whether you like it or not.'

photo: Stephen Cummiskey

George Devine, first artistic director of the English Stage Company: notes for an unwritten book.

As Britain's leading national company dedicated to new work, the Royal Court Theatre produces new plays of the highest quality, working with writers from all backgrounds, and addressing the problems and possibilities of our time.

"The Royal Court has been at the centre of British cultural life for the past 50 years, an engine room for new writing and constantly transforming the theatrical culture." Stephen Daldry

Since its foundation in 1956, the Royal Court has presented premieres by almost every leading contemporary British playwright, from John Osborne's Look Back in Anger to Caryl Churchill's A Number and Tom Stoppard's Rock 'n' Roll. Just some of the other writers to have chosen the Royal Court to premiere their work include Edward Albee, John Arden, Richard Bean, Samuel Beckett, Edward Bond, Leo Butler, Jez Butterworth, Martin Crimp, Ariel Dorfman, Stella Feehily, Christopher Hampton, David Hare, Eugène Ionesco, Ann Jellicoe, Terry Johnson, Sarah Kane, David Mamet, Martin McDonagh, Conor McPherson, Joe Penhall, Lucy Prebble, Mark Ravenhill, Simon Stephens, Wole Soyinka, Polly Stenham, David Storey, Debbie Tucker Green, Arnold Wesker and Roy Williams.

"It is risky to miss a production there." Financial Times

In addition to its full-scale productions, the Royal Court also facilitates international work at a grass-roots level, developing exchanges which bring young writers to Britain and sending British writers, actors and directors to work with artists around the world. The research and play development arm of the Royal Court Theatre, The Studio, finds the most exciting and diverse range of new voices in the UK. The Studio runs play-writing groups including the Young Writers Programme, Critical Mass for Black, Asian and minority ethnic writers and the biennial Young Writers Festival. For further information, go to www.royalcourttheatre.com/playwriting/the-studio.

Supported by
ARTS COUNCIL ENGLAND

ROYAL COURT SUPPORTERS

The Royal Court has significant and longstanding relationships with many organisations and individuals who provide vital support. It is this support that makes possible its unique playwriting and audience development programmes.

Coutts supports Innovation at the Royal Court. The Genesis Foundation supports the Royal Court's work with International Playwrights. Theatre Local is sponsored by Bloomberg. Alix Partners support The Big Idea at the Royal Court. The Jerwood Charitable Foundation supports emerging writers through the Jerwood New Playwrights series. The Andrew Lloyd Webber Foundation supports the Royal Court's Studio, which aims to seek out, nurture and support emerging playwrights. The Harold Pinter Playwright's Award is given annually by his widow, Lady Antonia Fraser, to support a new commission at the Royal Court.

Supported by
ARTS COUNCIL ENGLAND

Innovation Partner

Royal
Exchange
Theatre

Situated in the heart of Manchester, the Royal Exchange is one of the UK's leading producing theatres. We are home to two performance spaces: a 750-seat glass and steel in-the-round Theatre and a 100-seat flexible Studio space. We produce up to twelve productions a year alongside a diverse touring programme of work.

We nurture outstanding creative talent in our city and attract some of the most original artists and theatre makers in the country to present high quality classic plays and new writing to entertain, provoke and inspire. We provide opportunities for people of all ages, backgrounds and abilities to explore and develop their creative imaginations in our iconic building.

During the last ten years we have produced over fifty new plays across both our spaces and worked with a huge range of writers at different stages in their careers including Simon Stephens, Vivienne Franzmann, Simon Armitage, Alistair McDowall, Matthew Dunster, Chloe Moss and Duncan MacMillan. Most recently we produced the world premiere of *Blindsided* by Simon Stephens, and from 8 May–7 June we have the premiere of *The Last Days of Troy,* by Simon Armitage running in rep with the Bruntwood Prize-winning play *Britannia Waves The Rules* by Gareth Farr.

The Great Hall of the Royal Exchange

Royal Exchange Theatre, St. Ann's Square, Manchester, M2 7DH
www.royalexchange.co.uk +44 161 833 9333

To donate and find out more: royalexchange.co.uk/donate

AGMA
ASSOCIATION OF
GREATER MANCHESTER
AUTHORITIES

MANCHESTER
CITY COUNCIL

LOTTERY FUNDED

Supported using public funding by
**ARTS COUNCIL
ENGLAND**

ROYAL EXCHANGE THEATRE STAFF

Spring / Summer 2014

Exchange

Royal
Exchange
Theatre

Orlando
The Theatre Thu 20 Feb - Sat 22 Mar
From the novel by Virginia Woolf. Adaptation by Sarah Ruhl.
Directed by Max Webster. With Suranne Jones.

A Royal Exchange Theatre production

SOLD
OUT

Black Roses: The Killing of Sophie Lancaster
The Studio Wed 26 Feb - Sat 8 Mar
Words by Sylvia Lancaster. Poetry by Simon Armitage.
Directed by Sarah Frankcom and Susan Roberts.
The production supports the ongoing work of the **Sophie Lancaster Foundation**
(registered charity no. 1129689)

Much Ado About Nothing
The Theatre Thu 27 Mar - Sat 3 May
By William Shakespeare. Directed by Maria Aberg.

World Premiere
The Last Days of Troy
The Theatre Thu 8 May - Sat 7 Jun
By Simon Armitage. Directed by Nick Bagnall. With Lily Cole.

A Roundhouse production in partnership with Royal Exchange Theatre and Contact Theatre
(Manchester) and Cast (Doncaster)

Puffball
The Theatre Sun 8 and Mon 9 Jun
Directed by Mark Storor.

Billy Liar
The Theatre Fri 13 Jun - Sat 12 Jul
By Keith Waterhouse and Willis Hall. Directed by Sam Yates.

A Royal Exchange Theatre and New Vic Theatre, Newcastle under Lyme co-production

Around the World in Eighty Days
The Theatre Thu 17 Jul - Sat 16 Aug
Adapted by Laura Eason from the novel by Jules Verne.
Directed by Theresa Heskins.

Box Office 0845 450 4808 / royalexchange.co.uk/season

✖ Royal Exchange Theatre, St Ann's Square, Manchester M2 7DH

AGMA
ASSOCIATION OF
GREATER MANCHESTER
AUTHORITIES

MANCHESTER
CITY COUNCIL

Supported using public funding by
ARTS COUNCIL
LOTTERY FUNDED | **ENGLAND**

Registered charity
no. 255424

PESTS

Vivienne Franzmann

Author's Note

Over the last three years of working with Clean Break, I have met many women who are in prison or have been in prison. What I have learnt about how and why women end up in the criminal justice system is in this play.

Thank you to

The women I met in prisons. Your stories and your survival have moved me profoundly.

The women who attend Clean Break. It is amazing to be in a place where there is such optimism and hope, and you are responsible for that.

Everyone who works at Clean Break. I have felt your warmth and encouragement from the moment I entered the building. Every day you change people's lives, which is an incredible thing.

The Royal Exchange Theatre and the Royal Court Theatre for your support.

The production team on *Pests*. Big incredible creative brains.

Imogen Ashby for all the workshop stuff and the support and the massive laughs and the stories and the warm-ups and the ailments.

Lucy Morrison who has been there throughout, commissioning, supporting, encouraging, questioning, laughing, advising, creating, and discussing smallness. Thank you.

V.F.

4

Characters

PINK, *twenty-five years*
ROLLY, *twenty-one years*
UNKNOWN WOMAN

*At no point does Rolly ever experience the aural/visual images
that Pink sees and/or hears.*

*This text went to press before the end of rehearsals and so may
differ slightly from the play as performed.*

Scene One

*PINK's nest. One room. A state. Newspaper torn up and
shredded everywhere. A mattress slumped in the corner. A
yellowing duvet – shredded paper all over it. Stained sofa. Old
food. Cans. Sheets of newspaper randomly stuck up on some of
the walls with parcel tape. An old and battered telly in the
corner. The walls are streaked with blood/shit/food/who knows.
The Spice Girls' 'Wannabe' plays on a crappy CD player.*

*Knock on the door. Nothing. Another knock. Another. Nothing.
Louder. Much louder. From a pile of shredded newspapers, a
face darts out. This is* PINK. *Knock again.* PINK *looks worried.
Gets up, turns CD player off. A sequence of knocks. A secret
sequence.* PINK *goes to the door. Twitch. Smells the air. Opens
the door.* ROLLY *stands in the doorway, pregnant, with a plastic
bag in her hand. A pause.* PINK *stands to the side to let her in.*
ROLLY *walks in with her plastic bag, see-through, with just a
few belongings in it.* PINK *closes the door. She turns and looks
at* ROLLY. ROLLY *looks back.* PINK *walks up to* ROLLY.
They stand dead still, ready. ROLLY *moves backwards.* PINK
moves towards her. ROLLY *stands her ground.* PINK *stops.*
Suddenly, ROLLY *charges at* PINK. PINK *wrestles her to the
ground.* ROLLY *retaliates, flipping* PINK *over.* PINK *bites her
arm.* ROLLY *lets go.* PINK *legs it over the sofa.* ROLLY *pulls
her back.* PINK *tries to get away. She kicks* ROLLY *off.* ROLLY
grabs her by the hair. PINK *stops. They both freeze.*

PINK. Violationary.

> *Beat.*

> Rule breakage.

> *Beat.*

> Your lugs receivin' me?

> *Beat.*

Rule six of da code, never mawl da –

Beat.

Don't pretendy.

Beat.

Do not fuckin' pretendy. Release.

Beat.

Release da fur.

Beat.

I means it.

Beat.

I gettin'… I ain't jokin'. I…

Beat.

Vexationary… I is gettin'.

Beat.

Itchy…

Beat.

I warnin' you.

Beat.

Liberate.

Beat.

I is fuckin' warnin' you.

Beat.

Liberate.

Beat.

Or I tear your fuckin' tits off.

ROLLY *lets go.* PINK *straightens herself up. Pause.*
PINK *looks at* ROLLY.

(*Punches her on the arm.*) You is such a –

ROLLY (*punches her on the arm*). You is.

PINK (*punches her on the arm*). You is.

ROLLY. You is.

PINK. You fuckin' is.

Silence. They smile at each other. ROLLY *looks round
the room.*

ROLLY. Looks repeat, innit.

PINK (*motioning to the telly*). Apart from da goggle-box.

Beat.

Number four since –

ROLLY. Is it?

PINK. Got it, flogged it, got it, flogged it, got it, flogged it, got
it, keeped it.

ROLLY. How long you done keeped it?

PINK. Two weeks. It a record, huh? A fuckin' world record.
Enter me in da Guinness Book of World Records. 'Member
dat tome? Jayne an' Mike gived it you for Christmas.
'Member da world's biggest foots? Size thirty. Size fuckin'
thirty. Fuckin' clown foots. When you get out?

ROLLY. Yesterday.

PINK. Want summit to quench?

ROLLY. Nah, had a –

PINK. Munch?

ROLLY. Nah, I's –

PINK. You sure?

Pause.

A little gnaw?

ROLLY. No thanks.

Beat.

PINK. For real?

ROLLY. Yeah.

Beat.

PINK. Goods for you.

Beat.

Gold star.

ROLLY. Thanks.

PINK. For sure. Gold star.

Silence.

(*Indicating plastic bag.*) I like your bag.

ROLLY *looks at her.*

Is it one of dem Victoria Beckhams?

ROLLY *laughs.*

Spice up your life! Slice up your wife! Put up da price!
Wanna really really wanna wanna zig-a-zig-ah. Zig-a-zig-ah.
Zig-a-zig-ah. Where d'ya stay last night?

ROLLY. Nowhere.

PINK. Sounds nice.

Beat.

Zig-a-zig-ah. (*Motioning to* ROLLY'*s pregnancy.*) Swelled
up peachy now. 'Member how big I grewed wiv Tia. Could
hardly fuckin' wander by da ends.

ROLLY. Everyfing been alright? You been –

PINK. Yeah, cool.

ROLLY. You sure?

PINK. For sure. Everyfing's been coolness.

ROLLY. Cos when you dint come to seed me.

PINK. Yeah, 'pologetics 'bout dat –

ROLLY. I thinked maybe…

PINK. Nah.

Beat.

ROLLY. Good.

Beat.

I fretted up. I got all –

PINK. Wanna know what you's blinked an' missed?

Beat.

ROLLY. Yeah, g'on.

PINK. Arks me den.

ROLLY. What?

PINK. Arks me 'bout da happinins. It polite rah-rah to arks, innit.

Beat.

ROLLY. What done been da happinins?

PINK. Nah.

ROLLY. What?

PINK. Pink, dearest blood, who I missed wiv all my throbbin' heart, what been da happinins, please do telt, thanks very muchness.

Beat.

ROLLY. Pink, dearest blood, who I missed wiv…

PINK. All my throbbin' heart.

ROLLY. All my throbbin' heart.

PINK. What done been da happinins?

ROLLY. What done been da happinins?

PINK. Please do telt.

Beat.

ROLLY. Please do telt.

PINK. Thanks very muchness.

ROLLY. Thanks very muchness.

Pause. ROLLY *waits.*

PINK. Nuttin much.

ROLLY. Den why you make me –

PINK *grins.*

Bitch.

PINK *hums 'If I Only Had a Brain'.*

Fuckin' bitch.

Beat.

PINK. Slo Mo sexin' up on White Patch now.

ROLLY. Is it?

PINK. Small Foot gassed it. Mouth as big as a fuckin' watermelon. Never telt her nuttin unless you wan' it plagued round da whole colony in a nano. Unless you, like, wan' all dems to know 'bout dem zits on your bits an' your –

ROLLY. I ain't got no zits on my bits.

PINK. Ain't sayin' you have.

ROLLY. Good cos I ain't.

Pause.

Is it okay to for me to curl here?

Beat.

If it ain't convenience den I can always, you know, find nuva nest. I go arks down da stinkin' lanes.

PINK *smiles. Beat.*

Bitch.

PINK. As if you need to arks. As if you need to fuckin' arks.

The sun shines on PINK*'s face. She basks. Beat.*

ROLLY. You fuckin' bitch.

Beat.

You roarin' fuckin' bitch.

PINK *laughs.*

PINK. One-ball Johnny's got a jobbage.

ROLLY. Doin' what?

PINK. Clearin' gutters, diggin' holes, shreddin' shit. Dunno, somefing fuckin' borin'. Black Nose is still here. Been stayin' over by da gassy holes wiv de –

ROLLY. What 'bout Red-eyed Paul?

PINK. What 'bout him?

ROLLY. Just ponderin' if –

PINK *gets up and plays 'Wannabe' again.*

PINK. Why you ponderin' him for?

ROLLY. You seed him?

PINK. Nah, not in ages.

ROLLY. When in ages?

PINK. Dunno.

Pause.

ROLLY. What did he chat?

PINK. What?

ROLLY. When you seed him?

PINK. Nuttin.

ROLLY. Did he chat ting 'bout me?

Beat.

PINK. You is very narcissistic.

ROLLY. What?

PINK. You got egotistical qualitities.

Beat.

We done don't waste all our whole completed lives chewin' over you.

ROLLY. I never –

PINK. Not every yah-de-yah has your name bouncin' through it like a ping-pong.

Beat.

Da wheel ain't stop turnin' just cos you been gone.

Beat.

Da rivers still flow an' the monkeys still fuck in da trees.

Beat.

Life carries on, you get me?

Beat.

ROLLY. I jus' –

PINK. We still clawin', grazin', scrapin', gnawin'. We is –

ROLLY. But what 'bout Red-eye?

PINK. What 'bout him?

ROLLY. When I wasn't never here, what did he –

PINK. You is scratchin' at my tits. You is –

ROLLY. Cos I owed him.

Beat.

PINK. It paid.

ROLLY. What?

PINK. I paid him all up.

Beat.

Borrowed off Major Tail.

ROLLY. But it –

PINK. Paid him back installiments. Monthie by monthie.

Beat.

ROLLY. I never done meant it for youse to –

PINK. It nuttin.

ROLLY. I give you da greens, I –

PINK. No necessitation.

ROLLY. But I wanna –

PINK. No fuckin' necessitation.

ROLLY. But –

PINK. Everyfing is coolness.

Beat.

Now, create me a cup of Yorkshire, you lazy flea-infested skank.

Beat. ROLLY *gets up.*

ROLLY. We got any tea bags?

PINK. Yeah.

ROLLY. Where?

PINK. Where dey always is, sista.

The sun glows, children giggle. PINK *basks. Happy.*

Where dey always is, innit.

Scene Two

PINK *and* ROLLY *on the sofa. Nesting material all over them. Watching telly –* Life of Grime/How Clean is Your House?-*type thing. A row of medicine bottles in front of them.* ROLLY *takes two pills out each time; one for her, one for* PINK. ROLLY *has a cup of tea and* PINK *a can of beer.*

PINK (*motioning at the telly*). I don't approve of dis show. I for sure don't fuckin' approve. Dese folk ain't wellage.

Beat. ROLLY *takes her pill and hands over the other to* PINK.

Dey's at severest disadvantage, innit. Look at her. Fuck's sake. Look at her fur. She ain't groomed dat fur in… never… She ain't never groomed dat fur. The last time she had a shampoo an' blow-dry was, like, never.

Beat. ROLLY *takes another.*

She can't even converse proper. Just done mumble an' stare down at da dust. (*Takes it.*) She don't even make da eyeballs contact. Bet she autistic, bet she got Asperger's or summit…

ROLLY *hands one to* PINK.

Dis is shit, man. Seaside circus freakage. Poor dafty.

Silence. They watch. ROLLY *looks at the last bottle. She takes one pill and puts the lid on.* PINK *looks at her.*

ROLLY. For my liver, innit.

PINK *shrugs, takes the bottle, takes one out and swallows it.*

PINK. Can just imaginate it, innit, all dem tv nobs sittin' round
wiv dere Pret-a-Mange free-rangey baguettes an' Flatish
Whites, 'Oh I know a filthy fruit bat who resides in da
council 'state at da end of my road. She ain't been out da
house fifteen years since the death of her beloved mother.
Let us propel a camera crew round an' get her to sprucify it
all up, honestly, it'll transformify da scuzzy dirtbag's life,
literally, like, literally like literally, like completely literally
an' we'll be dere to catch it all, as an' when, as an' when, as
an' when, honestly, literally, like, literally.' (*Motions at pills.*)
What else you hoardin'?

ROLLY. Dat's it.

PINK *reaches over and takes* ROLLY*'s asthma pump.*

PINK. Fuckin' liar.

PINK *does three quick puffs on the inhaler.*

Where your juice?

ROLLY. All out.

Beat.

Goin' da doctor man in a bit.

Beat.

PINK. Well, dat is bangin' nice, don't considerate moi, will ya?

ROLLY. But you wasn't here –

PINK. Still though. Still.

ROLLY. You's all crammed up from Tiny's –

PINK. Yeah, but a little top-up would've been flavoursome, innit.

ROLLY *looks through the bottles left on the table.*

ROLLY. Where's your –

PINK. Stopped takin' it.

Beat.

Never needed it no more.

ROLLY. Yeah?

PINK. Make me all swelled up like a fatty.

ROLLY. But –

PINK. Make me all dulled an' grey.

ROLLY. But –

PINK. Dat all over wiv now.

ROLLY. But –

PINK. Dun an' dusted.

ROLLY. But if you –

PINK *silences her with a hand.*

PINK. Dun an' dirt dusted.

Pause.

(*Looking at telly.*) I is gonna make a complainage. Who you think I do dat to? What da bloke in charge of BBC?

ROLLY. Jeremy Clarkson.

PINK. He ain't in charge.

ROLLY. He done dat programme.

PINK. Yeah –

ROLLY. Wiv dat iccle one who got all blowed up all over da place an' lost half his brain cellage.

PINK. He dint lose half his brain.

ROLLY. Yeah, yeah his brain's all broke now.

PINK. Nah, he –

ROLLY. 'S called Hamster.

PINK. Hammond. Richard Hammond.

ROLLY. Nah, it ain't.

PINK. Hamster his nickiname.

ROLLY. He well tinied.

PINK. Yeah, like a hamster.

ROLLY. Like a Lilliputian.

PINK. A what?

ROLLY. A Lilliputian.

PINK. A lilly fuckin' what?

ROLLY. *Gulliver's Travels*, innit. 'S a book ting. 'S like a midget or somefing. A munchkin, an Oompa Loompa ting.

Beat.

Had a mate, she readed stuff an' dat.

PINK. Yeah?

ROLLY. At night, she readed books out an' ting.

Beat. PINK *starts laughing.*

PINK. She telt you da bedtime stories?

ROLLY. It weren't like dat. It weren't –

PINK. Did she flannel your face an' wipe your bot-bot an' all.

Beat.

Iccle baby. Like a iccle baby.

Beat.

Muppet. Iccle baby fuckin' muppet.

Silence.

ROLLY. Could be Fiona Bruce.

Beat.

She dat one on da *Antiques Roadshow.*

PINK. I know who Fiona Bruce is.

ROLLY. Love dat show. Love their faces when –

PINK. It worth fuck-all. Innit. 'Member Maureen? She went on it an' –

ROLLY. Nah, love it when it worth all da greens.

Darkness in the corner of the room. A beat. PINK *looks. The darkness makes its way towards her. She watches it. She gets up and turns on the CD player – 'Wannabe'.*

When dey got it at car-boot an' it a Ming. Or a bit of sewin' or whatever an' it turnt out Queen Victoria's nanny dun it.

The darkness moves away.

Or a picture dat dey teared da back off an' dere anuva underneath an' it a modern classic of a Cornish beach scene.

Beat.

Yeah, a modern classic, innit.

Pause. The darkness fades. PINK *turns the CD off. Silence.*

PINK. Did you used to goggle it when you was at Jayne an' Mike's?

Beat.

Did you done goggle it at –

ROLLY. Nah.

PINK. Bet you did.

ROLLY. Dint.

PINK. I bet it was total per cent da sort of ting dey goggled, Jayne an' Mike. Bet dey lugged da *Archers* an' all.

ROLLY. I reckons Fiona Bruce proper nice wiv her pups. Firm but fairage.

PINK. How do you know she got pups?

ROLLY. Everyone got pups, innit.

Silence. ROLLY *gets up and pulls on a coat.*

PINK. Hold up, I come wiv ya.

Beat.

What, you don't want me to?

ROLLY. Nah, nah, I ain't never gonna be long, just –

PINK. Just what?

ROLLY. Thought… Thought I –

PINK. Fuck off an' leave me here all Hans Solo. On me Jack Jones, totally Toblerone, hangin' on da telephone.

Pause. PINK *smiles.*

ROLLY. Bitch.

PINK *pulls* ROLLY *towards her.* PINK *puts her arms round her.*

PINK (*sings from* The Wizard of Oz). I'd while away da hours –

ROLLY. Yeah, I done got get scurryin' –

PINK (*sings*). Conferrin' wiv da flowers –

ROLLY. Da appointment's at –

PINK *holds on to her.*

PINK (*sings*). Consultin' wiv da rain. (*Beat.*)

An' my head, I'd be scratchin' while –

Beat. PINK *gestures to* ROLLY. *Nothing.*

My thoughts I'd be hatchin'.

PINK *gestures for her to get involved. Beat.*

ROLLY (*reluctantly sings*). If I only had a brain.

A kite floats. PINK *looks up and smiles. Beat.*

PINK. Yeah? Yeah?

Beat.

ROLLY. Yeah.

PINK. Fetch chocelat when you's out. Double Decker. An' if you near Fat Tony's, can you telt him dat –

ROLLY. I ain't travellin' Fat Tony's vicinity.

PINK. Yeah, da doctor man is steps from his nest.

ROLLY. Nah, it –

PINK. Telt him I got da greens, just waitin' on Dregs, owes me, innit.

ROLLY. I don't wanna –

PINK. Only take you –

ROLLY. It ain't good for me.

PINK. Fuck's sake.

Silence. Kite swirls. Darkening. White noise. PINK *quickly gets her coat and gets her keys. She heads to the door.*

Let's get scuttlin'.

Beat.

C'mon, what you waitin' for?

Scene Three

PINK *is pulling out loads of different clothes with tags on them from her coat/tracksuit/bag. As she talks, she looks at the labels to see how much each one is worth and chucks them on the sofa. The pile grows. When she's finished, she pulls out a bottle of vodka.* ROLLY *lies in the nest.*

PINK. An' Matey Katey's all, 'I give you a blow job if you seed me right.' An' she on her knees an' Tom Tom's all, 'You a sket, a manky sket. I prefer a blow job off dat fat boy off *X Factor* dan you.' An' all de while she takin' her teeth out. An' Tom Tom's makin' puke-up faces. An' dere dis massive crashage an' Hairy Harry's chokin' up da doorway, all trogladyte, proper he-man and everyone's all –

ROLLY. You eyeballed my beep?

PINK. What?

ROLLY. My beep.

PINK *gets* ROLLY*'s phone out of her pocket and hands it to her. Pause.*

PINK. Pawed it by accident. Thinked it mine.

ROLLY *takes it, glances at it and puts it down.*

Dey was questionin' 'bout you.

Beat.

Minin' to know why you ain't been round.

Beat.

Told 'em you was off da gnaw.

Beat.

Dey telt good for you.

Beat.

Honest, dat's what dey telt. Gold star. (*Beat.*) What is dat ringtone?

ROLLY. A hip-hop chicken.

PINK. It fuckin' embarrassin'. Change it.

ROLLY. I like it.

PINK. It a iccle pup ting, for da babies. (*Finds her own phone, plays it – 'All the Single Ladies'*.) It a classic. A fuckin' classic. May calt you.

Beat.

She lefted a message.

Beat.

It on dere. Da message.

Beat.

Ain't you gonna lug it?

Beat.

ROLLY. Yeah, laters.

PINK. Might be extra important.

Pause.

G'on.

Beat. PINK goes up and puts the phone in ROLLY's hand. ROLLY listens to the message. PINK watches her. She puts the phone down.

Who da fuck is May?

ROLLY. Just a mate.

PINK. You ain't never speaked of her.

Beat.

I mean, dat is a bit sus, you gotta concede. She your mate but you ain't never telt nuttin 'bout her. Not one ting. I chat shit 'bout Big Mal, Slo Mo, Black Nose, all dem, all da times, innit. But you ain't never done once telt nuttin 'bout dis May. Not a whisperage.

Beat.

What sort of name is dat anyways. May?

ROLLY. Dunno.

PINK. Granny, innit. She an old one?

ROLLY. Nah.

Pause.

PINK. So?

ROLLY. She just a mate.

PINK. An' what's da hotel she chattin' on 'bout?

Pause. ROLLY *looks at her.*

I done thought it might be a catastrophe. She runged five times.

Pause.

Well?

Beat.

ROLLY. She toils dere.

PINK. And?

ROLLY. Dere dis job ting dere.

A flame appears on the floor. PINK *moves to the CD player and plays 'Wannabe' quietly. She looks at the flame. It stays the same. She turns up the volume. The same. She moves to the flame and stands on it to extinguish it.*

Dere dis jobbage in dis hotel. In dis hotel, dis place where –

PINK. Where is it, dis hotel?

ROLLY. Harpenden.

PINK. Harpenden?

ROLLY. Yeah.

PINK. Where da fuck is Harpenden?

ROLLY. Hertfordshire.

PINK. Where da fuck is Hertfordshire?

ROLLY. Outside London.

Another flame appears. PINK *moves to it.*

It like countryside. It like –

PINK. Full of wankers, da countryside.

Beat.

All shootin' animals. Or if dey ain't shootin' da animals, dey's fuckin' 'em. Badgers an' dat.

Beat.

ROLLY. It just a brainwave, a liccle bulb, it –

PINK. Don't you have to be able to do da letters an' da adds up to toil in a hotel?

ROLLY. It cleanin'.

PINK. Yeah, but still.

ROLLY. An' I know a bit of my numbers now.

Beat.

PINK. Do ya?

Pause.

Four plus eight.

Beat.

ROLLY. Twelve.

PINK. Christ, it Carol fuckin' Vorderman.

Beat.

Notify Mensa, dere a new pup in town. Eight times seven.

Silence.

'Member when I had dat jobbage?

Beat.

It was shit.

Beat.

It shit havin' people teltin' you what to do all day. An' how to
act. An' when you can have your munch or your fag or a piss
or whatevers. An' all da other does are bitches, who chat dick
'bout you behind your fur an' den arks you if you wanna go
for a drink after workage an' try to fuck your boyfriend an'
den telt everyone he got a tiny weeny member. An' you have
to get up itchy early. An' you get home suckered late in da
black. An' you can't do what you wanna do. It ain't nice. It
ain't nice or good or fun or any of doze things.

ROLLY. I don't 'member you havin' no jobbage.

A flame. Beat.

PINK (*points at* ROLLY*'s belly*). What you gonna do 'bout –

ROLLY. I can take it wiv me.

PINK. What, you gonna strap it up on your back? Dis ain't
fuckin' Uganda. Strap it on while you scrub up bogs an'
hoover confetti puke? Dis ain't –

ROLLY. May's got a pup.

Beat.

An' a flat.

Beat.

She telt I can nest wiv her. We help each other. Share equal
da childcare an' dat.

PINK. Share equal da childcare? When done you get so fuckin'
middle class? What, you gonna get a nanny next? Gonna
start quaff quaffin' red wines an' chattin' shit 'bout dem
rocketin' house prices?

ROLLY. I look after hers when she toilin' an' –

PINK. Sounds cosy. Sounds right fuckin'cosy.

A flame.

Dere is people wiv university degrees an' shit who can't get
no job at da minute. Wiv PHDs toilin' in Pizza Huts or
Nando's. You ain't exactly –

ROLLY. Hotel take sorts like us.

Beat.

'S like a scheme or somefing. Like a… called a Second Chance Scheme.

Beat.

Da owner, he set it up… he wants to give sorts like us a second chance.

Beat.

PINK. Sorts like us? He takin' da fuckin' piss.

A flame.

Who is dis May?

ROLLY. She bona fide nice.

Beat.

She proper real kindness.

PINK. And?

Beat.

ROLLY. She a veganist.

Beat.

She done don't eat meat or eggs or –

PINK. I know what a veganist is.

ROLLY. An' she a paganist.

PINK. Christly God, you know how to pick 'em.

ROLLY. She had this… whassissname… yeah… shit, she told me da name… Altar! Dat's it. She had a altar in da cell. Used to say prayers, do chants an' stuff, like dat lady Mum used to –

PINK. She a witch. She a fuckin' witch.

ROLLY. She only nineteen, but she –

PINK. She a witch, Sabrina da Teenage Witch wiv her cat cault Salem an' her cunt-faced kid cault Abracadabra.

Pause.

ROLLY. Paganism ain't witchcraft.

PINK. I don't give a fuckism what it ain't.

Pause.

ROLLY. May telt da test was easy so I thinked –

PINK. You gotta take a test, like exam ting?

ROLLY. I dunno, yeah, s'pose.

PINK. You gotta sit down an' take a –

ROLLY. I dunno if you sit down.

PINK. But you gotta pass a test?

ROLLY. Yeah, everyone does.

PINK. Like a readin' ting?

ROLLY. Dunno.

The flames extinguish by themselves. Silence.

PINK. If you really wanna go be dere, I fink you should.

Beat.

It a fresh start, innit.

ROLLY. Dat's what I done thought.

PINK. A spring fresh start.

Beat.

I worried 'bout ya, 's all.

Beat.

An' I miss ya already.

ROLLY. I miss ya already too.

PINK. I miss ya real bad.

ROLLY. I miss ya real bad backatcha.

PINK. But you can come back visit on your spare day, innit.

ROLLY. I ain't got no jobbage yet.

PINK. You gotta fink pluses not minuses.

Beat.

ROLLY. I ain't gonna win it.

PINK. Pluses finking will support you.

ROLLY. Wiv my readin' an' my numbers an' dat, I won't –

PINK. You get dat jobbage.

ROLLY. But what if dey arks me questions?

PINK. What?

ROLLY. In da fing… in da interview fing.

PINK. Dat's what interview is. Questions.

ROLLY. But what if I can't answer 'em all tiptop?

PINK. You will.

ROLLY. But, what if –

PINK. You can practise.

Beat.

ROLLY. Practice make perfect, innit.

PINK. Yeah.

Beat.

ROLLY. Dat's what Jayne used to telt. When she tooked me to dem dancy lessons in dat churchy hall.

Silence.

May telt it so black in da countryside dat you can't even seed your paw in front of your schnoze.

Pause.

What if I have to stroll 'bout in da black?

Beat.

What if I heared an owl an' I'm all asnooze an' I dunno what
it is an' I get up to seed an' I'm all hazy dreamlike an' I
stumble out of da flat, da sharin' flat, da flat I share wiv May,
an' I goes down da road all half-asnooze an' I awake in da
middle of a field, in da blackest black wiv nothing dere 'cept
an owl eyeballin' me, eyeballin' right in my face, right in my
face wiv its ginormous owl eyes, not blinkin'.

Beat.

PINK. Dat ain't goin' to happen.

ROLLY. But what if –

PINK. You can acquire a torch an' shine it at da owl till he fly
away. (*Beat.*) Ring May an' telt her you up for it.

ROLLY. But what I –

PINK. Ring her.

ROLLY. How will I get dere?

PINK. On a choo.

ROLLY. What if I get lost?

PINK. Den you done arks someone s–o–s.

ROLLY. Will you come wiv me?

PINK *opens her hands, white sand pours on to the floor
through her fingers. She watches.*

I don't wanna go on me jacks.

PINK. You be all good. Don't fret.

ROLLY. But –

PINK. You be gold star.

Scene Four

ROLLY *has a bin bag and is tidying up the flat. She makes her way round methodically, humming as she goes, taking pleasure.* PINK *comes in and slams the door behind her. She goes straight to the pills.*

PINK. Dat cunt, dat champin' dirty lice-infested bastard.

> ROLLY *barely looks up. She carries on cleaning.*

Took me for a muggins. Telt me I only gaved him five. Bullshit. Gaved him twenty. Gaved him a fuckin' twenty.

She takes out some pills, knocks them back.

Telt him, 'I'm comin' back. Gonna get Black Nose an' Slo Mo an' come back for da extra. Wot I'm owed.' Just chuckled at me. Fuckin' chuckled. Gobbed in his cancer face. Soon stopped his fuckin' chuckles. Hightailed it out of his den, quickly quick like a bomb up ma woo-woo. Fuckin' ruffle me. Fuckin tryin' to ruffle me.

> ROLLY *picks up the bottles and puts them back in the right place. She carries on tidying up.* PINK *watches her.*

What you doin'?

Beat.

> Oi, Kim an' Aggie tits, what you doin'?

ROLLY. Tidyin'.

PINK. What for?

ROLLY. Feelded like it.

> *A beat.* PINK *starts picking rubbish up and putting it in the bin bag that* ROLLY*'s holding.*

PINK. Dat stinkin' shitball.

ROLLY. I gotta get some tidy-tidy practice in.

PINK. Only gaved me fiver's 'mount.

ROLLY. For my interview.

Beat.

Next week.

Beat.

Done got interview next week. At da –

PINK (*tidying*). Telt him 'Dat ain't gonna seed me right for five
  minutes, how ma gonna fill my veins wiv dat?' He telt, 'I
  don't give a pigeon's eggy shit. You gaved me five.' What a
  liar. Fuckin' junkie liar.

ROLLY. You want some brekkie?

Beat.

I could conjure us a bit of da hot stuff.

Beat.

A bit of frying up.

PINK. Frying up?

ROLLY. Or somefing.

PINK. Or somefing?

ROLLY. Yeah, why not?

Beat.

PINK. What is this, Gordon Ramsay's den?

ROLLY. Just thought I could –

PINK. Oh my days, he dint rock up in your prison an' all?

ROLLY. What?

PINK. Gordon Ramsay.

ROLLY. What 'bout him?

PINK. He done dat fing on da goggle-box, roared inside Brixton.

ROLLY. What for?

PINK. Mend all da depraved bucks wiv his cookin'.

Beat.

Teached 'em right from wrong through da bakin'.

Beat.

ROLLY. Did it work?

PINK. Dunno, never goggled all of it, he a wanker, innit.

Beat.

ROLLY. I got some oink if you wanna sangwhich.

Beat.

You sit down. I conjure it all up.

PINK. Rather do this.

As she's tidying, PINK *pulls a book,* The Wizard of Oz, *out from under the mattress. A beat. She looks at it. She looks at* ROLLY, *who quickly gets on with the tidying.*

Beat.

What dis?

PINK *shows it to* ROLLY. *A beat.* ROLLY *takes it from her.*

ROLLY. It was gonna be a bombshell.

Beat.

I was gonna bombshell you.

Beat.

I's learnin'.

Beat.

I done been learnin'.

Beat.

PINK. An' you can...

ROLLY. Yeah, a liccle, a –

PINK. A liccle?

ROLLY *nods.* PINK *motions for her read something. Beat.*

ROLLY. I ain't very gold star.

PINK. Don't matter.

ROLLY. It all a bit… you know…

PINK. What?

ROLLY. Uphill.

Beat.

PINK. Who taught ya?

ROLLY. May.

PINK. Veganist, paganist, now teacherist.

ROLLY (*reading in a halting, childlike way*). Dorothy lived in the midst of the great Kansas Prairies, with Uncle Henry, who was a farmer and Aunt Em who was the farmer's wife.

PINK. Fuck, my bonce is splittin'.

ROLLY. Their house was small, for the lumber to build it had to be carried by wagon many –

PINK (*taking the book from* ROLLY *and chucking it to the side*). You right, you ain't much good.

A pause. ROLLY *goes back to tidying.*

What is da pointation of this? What is da fuckin' – ? It a plague pit. Da whole place is stink. Make me puke nestin' here. Can't stand it… Can't fuckin' stand it.

PINK *grabs the bin bag from her.* PINK *dumps all the rubbish back on the floor. And lies down on the sofa. Silence.* ROLLY *starts picking it all up again. Silence.*

Sorry.

Beat.

Your lugs open?

Beat.

You s'posed to telt, 'it alright'. Dat what you's s'posed to telt. Telt 'it don't matter'.

Beat.

G'on.

Beat.

Telt it.

Beat.

ROLLY. It alright.

PINK. Like you means it.

Beat.

ROLLY. It alright.

PINK. I don't trust in you.

ROLLY. It is, it alright.

PINK. But you ain't teltin' like you –

ROLLY. How am I s'posed to –

PINK. From da throbbin' heart.

Beat.

From in dark deep, from –

ROLLY. I forgived you.

Beat.

PINK. Dat fuckin' gougin' pit face. Teltin' me I only gaved him five.

ROLLY *keeps clearing up.* PINK *lies on the sofa. A darkness travels through the room. A noise – heightened noise of* ROLLY *cleaning up, becomes louder, laced with a rumbling, a growl, an approach.*

(*To* ROLLY.) Stop doin' dat.

ROLLY *carries on.*

Cease it.

Beat.

It makin' me all…

Beat.

It makin' me feeled…

Beat.

It makin' my brains all…

Beat.

Stop fuckin' doin' dat.

ROLLY *stops. She looks at* PINK.

(*Watching the darkness approaching her.*) Jesus.

PINK *quickly gets up and moves towards the CD player. She presses it to play. It doesn't work. She presses it again.* ROLLY *watches her.* PINK *presses it over and over again, all the time turning to see the darkness approaching.*

Where da – ?

ROLLY *looks where* PINK *is looking. She doesn't see anything.*

Where da zig-a-zig-ah?

Beat.

Where da fuck is da zig-a-zig-ah?

ROLLY *moves over to the CD player. She gently moves* PINK *out of the way and takes the CD out. She wipes it.*

Fuck.

ROLLY *puts it back in the CD player. She presses play. Doesn't work. Presses again. Doesn't work.*

What we gonna do? What da fuck we –

PINK *keeps looking towards the darkness.* ROLLY *watches* PINK *watching the darkness as it is almost upon her.* PINK *turns away and puts her hands over her ears.*

Jesus, Mary, Joseph, Allah, Muhammad, Shiva, Jesus, Mary, Joseph.

She squeezes herself into the corner and closes her eyes. ROLLY *watches her.*

Zig-a-zig-ah.

Beat.

Zig-a-zig-ah.

Beat.

Zig-a-zig-ah.

The darkness and growl is upon PINK. *She stands in the furthest corner of the room.*

ROLLY *approaches* PINK *slowly. She gently takes* PINK*'s hands from her ears and holds her tightly.*

ROLLY (*quietly sings*). I'd while away da hours –
Conferrin' wiv da flowers
Consultin' wiv da rain. (*Beat.*)

And my head, I'd be scratchin' while –
My thoughts I'd be hatchin'.
If I only had a brain.

PINK *opens her eyes. The darkness and the noise recedes to a low hum.* PINK *recovers herself. Pause. She moves away.* ROLLY *watches her.*

PINK. Dat fuckin' mugster only givin' me five. Dat ruffler. Fuckin' tryin' to ruffle me.

Scene Five

PINK *is sitting on the sofa. She has a handbag and purse, not hers. She goes through the purse, sorting out the money. Chucks both to the side when she's done.* ROLLY *sits next to her. Dressed slightly better than usual.*

ROLLY. You never done believe who I eyeballed dere.

PINK. Ernest Hemingway.

ROLLY. Jenny Fingers.

Beat.

Yep.

PINK. Jenny Fingers?

ROLLY. Yeah.

PINK. Jenny Greasy Fingers?

ROLLY. Yep.

PINK. What she doin' dere?

ROLLY. She graftin' dere. Graftin' on da bar.

PINK. Gluggin' da bar, more like.

ROLLY. Nah, she given up da piss.

PINK. Yeah, right.

ROLLY. She don't drink nuttin.

PINK. Dat's her fairytale an' she stickin' to it.

ROLLY. She goes AA.

PINK. Yeah, seed how long dat lasts.

ROLLY. Been goin' ages.

PINK. Well, we can all goes AA, ain't meanings dat –

ROLLY. She been dry two years.

PINK. Bet she still gnawin' an' borin'.

ROLLY. She done goes NA an' all.

PINK. Surprised she got time to go toilin'.

ROLLY. She says da toil at da hotel's easiness.

Beat.

It is da toil on yourself dat is da toughness.

PINK. Fuckin' hell. She been gogglin' Oprah or what?

ROLLY. She got her pups back. Tommy an' Madison.

Silence.

PINK. How dat test went?

ROLLY. Easiness.

*A trickle of blood begins to slowly run down the wall that
PINK is facing.*

Was just 'bout what you would do if dere was a blaze an'
dat. Or a complainage. Or you founded a stuffed purse,
tings like dat.

PINK *turns away from the wall. She does not turn to face the
wall at any point in the scene, but can feel what is happening
behind her.*

PINK. What did dey arks in da interview?

ROLLY. Loads.

Beat.

Why I wanted da jobbage and –

PINK. What did you telt?

ROLLY. Telt dem I like da cleanin'.

Beat.

Arksed me if I was done ready to make dem changes in
my life.

PINK. Dey arksed you dat?

ROLLY. Arksed 'bout Mum an' Dad an' all.

PINK. Why did dey arks dat?

ROLLY. Telt somefing 'bout... dunno... can't 'member.

PINK. What did you telt dem?

ROLLY. All of it.

Beat.

PINK. Bet dey loved it.

ROLLY. Nah, dey –

PINK. Alkie nutnutjob dad, piss, shit, punch, junkie mum, no
    shoes, lice, black eye, care, fucked, excluded, bullied, foster
    home, gnaw, prison, gnaw, prison, gnaw, prison. 'Oh my gosh,
    it must have been so terrible for you. I can't imagine what it
    must have been like to have been born into a life of such
    deprivational violence. Horrifying. Absolute horrification.'

Silence.

    Did you telt dem 'bout Jayne an' Mike?

ROLLY. Yeah.

PINK. An' 'bout me.

ROLLY. Yeah.

PINK. 'Bout me nestin' at da home when you was nestin' wiv
    Jayne an' Mike.

ROLLY. Yeah.

PINK. What did you –

ROLLY. Telt dem we was separated.

PINK. For four years.

ROLLY. Yeah.

PINK. Dat I only came visited at Christmas an' birthdays.

ROLLY. Dat I missed you.

PINK. I was only allotted visitation at Christmas an' birthdays.

Beat.

Cos Jayne never keen on me.

ROLLY. She was, she –

PINK. Not enough.

Silence.

Did you telt dem 'bout our song?

Pause.

Why not?

Beat.

Did you telt dem 'bout da men?

Beat. Another trickle of blood.

Did you telt dem 'bout da men dat used to come to da home?

Beat.

When you was done all tucked up snug at Jayne and Mike's an' I was at da home.

Beat.

Did ya?

Beat.

Did you telt dem 'bout da men dat came wiv da Mars bars an' da Silk Cuts an' da teddy bears an' da pound coins?

Pause.

Why not?

ROLLY. Cos dat's your tale, innit.

Silence.

PINK. How many of you's dere?

ROLLY. Three.

PINK. How many jobs?

ROLLY. Three.

A trickle of blood. Beat.

PINK. An' da boss man interview you, yeah?

ROLLY. He not really da boss. I mean, he not really named dat. He more like a... I dunno...

PINK. So da boss man dint interview you?

ROLLY. Yeah, he did, wiv his wife, but it ain't not really like that.

Beat.

Like you know at school, dere da headmaster an' dat an' he in charge, an' he got his own room an' you got to knocky knock on da door, yeah?

PINK. Yeah.

ROLLY. An' you have to stand up till he telts you sit down. An' you have to tucked your shirt in an' he arks why you ain't got no tie an' why your shirt is all dirty plagued an' you ain't got no answer an' he gets angryfied an' he gets dat fing under his eye, dat fing he always gets, an' he arks why you punch Sarah Farconie in her smirk dat morning time during register an' you ain't got no answer other than cos she a nastiness fuckin' bitch' an' he says 'dat language is not 'propriate for school' an' he make you stand, on your tired liccle legs, outside his door all day, yeah?

PINK. Yeah.

ROLLY. Well, it ain't like dat.

Beat.

Douglas ain't like dat.

PINK. Douglas?

ROLLY. He da buck in charge.

PINK. So, he da boss man?

ROLLY. Nah, he ain't.

PINK. What den?

ROLLY. He telt he was more, I dunno, part of da hotel
community. I dunno, it lugged good when he telt it, I ain't –

PINK. How old is he?

ROLLY. Old.

PINK. Old man?

ROLLY. Yeah.

PINK. Old pervy man?

ROLLY. Nah.

PINK. Old pervy man who try put his hand up between
your legs?

ROLLY. He got a wife.

PINK. As if dat make a difference.

ROLLY. Valerie. She loveliness. Val-er-rie.

Pause.

PINK. An' what else happened?

ROLLY. Dey gave us a tour. Den we munched lunch.

PINK. What did you swallow?

ROLLY. Salmon. It a fish.

PINK. I know it a –

ROLLY. An' den for afters da main munch, we glugged coffee.

PINK. You don't like coffee.

A trickle of blood.

You done despise coffee.

ROLLY. Yeah, but –

PINK. You don't even tolerate da stink of it.

ROLLY. Wanted to give it goes.

PINK. You telt it bring you up in da pukes.

ROLLY. Yeah, but dis was alright –

PINK. Dat coffee cake I conjured wiv Maureen, I gave you slices. Brought it round to you at Jayne an' Mike's. You telt –

ROLLY. Yeah but –

PINK. You telt you was gonna splurge.

ROLLY. Yeah –

PINK. An' you gobbed it out in dat patio fing where you all sittage.

ROLLY. I was only ten.

PINK. An' den Timmy, dat West Highland terrier wiv da shitty arsehole, guzzled it all upped an' Mike maded dat ha ha ha 'bout Timmy havin' sophisticated taste an' dat he be arksin' for a cigar after dinner next. An' you all chuckled up. An' I went back to da home.

Silence.

ROLLY (*gets a posh biscuit out of her bag*). Got you dis.

ROLLY *hands it to* PINK.

I arksed if I could taked it. I dint just taked it.

A trickle of blood.

PINK. An' what now?

ROLLY. I gonna have a snooze.

PINK. 'Bout da jobbage?

ROLLY. Douglas gonna ring in a few days, let us know how it went.

Beat.

PINK. Funny name. Douglas.

ROLLY. Dat's what I telt.

PINK. Bet he dint like dat. Bet he –

ROLLY. Nah, he chuckled up proper like.

Pause.

(*Motioning to the nest.*) I just gonna –

PINK. Don't you give a shit pellet what I been up to?

ROLLY. Oh yeah, I was gonna arks –

PINK. Scratched over Tiny's nest an' Black Nose turned up wiv Grimes and he telt me dat last week, he –

ROLLY *yawns.* PINK *stops.*

ROLLY. Sorry… I's melted… I…

PINK *waves her away.* ROLLY *goes over to the nest, buries into it.* PINK *sits, she turns and stares at the wall. Blood trickles down it. She gets up. She gets a piece of newspaper and packing tape from the side and sticks the paper over it. It seeps through. She gets another sheet and does the same. It seeps through. She gets another. And again and again until it is covered. She sits down. A long time. She looks at* ROLLY*'s bag. She turns to look at the nest. She looks over at the paper. Blood seeps through.*

Scene Six

PINK *getting ready to go out*. ROLLY *motionless on sofa*.

Sounds of the sea, waves on a beach.

PINK. You total like sure?

> *Beat*.

> Make you feel improved.

> *Beat*.

> C'mon, rub eyeballs wiv me at Tiny's after.

> *Beat*.

> He's got barrels of sauce off Charlie Tophead, we can –

ROLLY. Nah.

> *Beat*.

PINK. It ain't good for ya, sit around stewin' like a pear.

> *Pause*.

> Is it?

> *Beat*.

> I show you good times.

ROLLY. I don't want no good times.

PINK. Now, dat is just self-hatred, innit.

> *Pause*.

> I know you shocked an' disappointed an' right hacked off.

> *Beat*.

> But it ain't doin' you no positives, is it? Squattin' down here like Miss fuckin' Havisham.

> *Beat*.

> So, you never gotted no poxy jobbage?

> *Beat*.

Fuck 'em. Dat's what I telt.

Beat.

If dey can't perceive how gold star my sista is den fuckin' fuck 'em.

Beat.

Fuck 'em up da arsehole wiv a spiky stick.

ROLLY. Dere was three jobs.

PINK. Maybe dere wasn't three –

ROLLY. Dere was.

PINK. Maybe you never hearded right.

ROLLY. I did.

PINK. Maybe your understandation wasn't too –

Beat.

It ain't meant to be, dat's all.

ROLLY. Dere was three of us.

Beat.

PINK. You never knows what gonna happen.

Beat.

Someting will float to da top, I bet.

Beat.

You could jackpot da Lotto.

Beat.

Conquer *Britain's Got Talent*.

Beat.

Acquire a jobbage in Marks an' Spencer's. In da bra department. Measure posh ladies' tit-tats all day an' get a discount on da munch. Who yearns to toil in a crappy hotel in da midst of da shit-sticks anyway?

Beat.

ROLLY. He telt I wasn't suitabled to da place.

PINK. He a cunt.

ROLLY. Telt I wasn't ready.

PINK. Total cunt.

ROLLY. I thoughted he liked me.

PINK. Totally cuntish.

ROLLY. It only cleanin'.

PINK. Totalicious cuntface.

ROLLY. It only cleanin'. It only fuckin' –

PINK. Zig-a-zig-ah.

ROLLY. Cleanin'.

Beat.

PINK. Dere be other jobbages.

ROLLY. But this nook was –

PINK. I knows.

ROLLY. It was so –

PINK. I knows.

ROLLY. An' May toils –

PINK. Bitch.

ROLLY. Why you fink she won't –

PINK. She a bitch.

ROLLY. I trieded her ten times.

PINK. Fuckin' witchity bitch.

ROLLY. I runged her ten –

PINK. C'mon out. Package up our troubles in an old kitbag.
C'mon.

ROLLY stares off into the distance. Pause.

ROLLY. Somefing abomination happened, I feeled it.

*Beat. ROLLY gets up. Crackling, white noise, tap-tap on
a door.*

I gonna get de choo down Harpenden.

PINK. Yeah but –

White noise, tap-tap on a door.

ROLLY. She done cracked open a calamity.

PINK. Nah, she –

ROLLY. All mashed up and –

PINK. She ain't mashed –

ROLLY. Disastered.

PINK. That ain't it.

ROLLY. Her pup is sick ting or –

PINK. Her pup's fine.

ROLLY. She might –

PINK. Everyfing's fine.

Beat.

Trust.

Pause.

ROLLY (*going to door*). Nah, I –

*White noise, tap-tap on the door. Door opening, keys thrown
down on a dresser.*

PINK (*quickly*). I speaked to her.

ROLLY. What?

PINK. I speaked to May.

Beat.

I runged her.

ROLLY. You runged May?

PINK. Yeah.

ROLLY. My May?

PINK. Yeah.

ROLLY. Why?

PINK. Cos I wanted to maked sure it was all... dat da hotel was all done... you know...

ROLLY. Yeah?

PINK. I had vexation dat dat hotel wasn't... I dunno, just sounded too merrily merrily to be... I was fretted dey –

ROLLY. What did she chat?

Beat.

What did she chat to you?

PINK. She telt da hotel was all good, it was all –

ROLLY. What did she chat 'bout me?

Pause.

PINK. She telt she dint wanna seed you no more.

Beat.

She telt dat she dint thinked you was nourishin' for her.

Beat. Sounds recede.

Dat she dint thinked it was tiptop to have you round her pup.

ROLLY. She spoke dat?

PINK. Yeah.

ROLLY. Dat what she done spoke? Dat what she actually spoke?

PINK. Yeah.

Beat.

She arksed me to keep you furtherly further from her.

Silence.

I dint wanna have to telt you, but it better you's in da knowledge, ain't it?

Beat.

I's welled-up sorry. It stinks. It a stinkin' shitball, but maybe it better dis way.

Silence. PINK *gently goes up to* ROLLY *and puts her arms round her.*

(*Sings gently.*) When a man's an empty kettle
He should be on his mettle

ROLLY *shrugs her off.* PINK *puts her arms round her again.*

And yet I'm torn apart
Because I'm presumin'

ROLLY *pushes her away.* PINK *perseveres. She holds her tight so she can't get away.*

Dat I could be a human
If I only had a heart.

PINK *kisses her on the cheek.*

I be back soon as.

Beat.

Where's your beep?

Beat.

When you last have it?

Beat. PINK *goes over to the nest and rummages around.*
She finds the phone.

You should always done keep it in da same spot. Den
you knows where it is. Gotta get organised. Keeped on
top of fings.

Beat.

I place it here. Dis is your spot. Every times you use it,
putted it back here, yeah?

PINK *puts the phone on the spot.*

If you needs me, just ring out, yeah?

Beat.

Yeah?

Beat.

ROLLY. Yeah.

Waves on a sandy beach, stars in the night sky.

PINK. Don't sit here feelin' dogshit all on your own.

PINK *goes. Silence.* ROLLY *sits. She lies down on the sofa.*
She stares at the ceiling. She gets up and goes to her phone.
She picks it up, takes it back to the sofa and sits. She phones,
answer machine.

ROLLY. Wanted to telt dat I's sorry. Sorry dat you conceive I
ain't gold star enough to... I proper sorry, May... I am all
welled-up sorry... I is blue wiv sorrows dat I ain't a better
girl for you.

ROLLY *sits. She gets up to put the phone back in the right*
place. She goes to the table. She puts it down. As she does
so, she sees, amongst the debris, a wrap. She picks it up.
She puts it down quickly. She stares at it. A long time. She
quickly sits down at the sofa. She gets up and goes to the
wrap. She picks it up. She takes it to the sofa. She sits down.
She puts the wrap on the sofa. She looks at it. A long time.

She picks it up. She very carefully opens the wrap and looks at the contents. Heroin. She smells it. She looks at it. An old friend. She picks up her phone, thinks about phoning again, puts it down. She sits. She looks at the wrap. A long time. She goes to a drawer and pulls out a spoon, a syringe, a belt and a lighter. Brings it back to the sofa. She sits. She rolls up her sleeve.

Scene Seven

PINK *and* ROLLY *are staring at a juicer on the table. The telly's gone. The place is a wreck; drug shit everywhere.*

ROLLY. What is it?

PINK. A juicer.

ROLLY. A what?

PINK. A fuckin' juicer.

ROLLY. A fuckin' juicer?

PINK. We need to ring up da changes, innit.

Beat.

Yeah, it all gettin' a bit, a bit. It all…

Beat.

Don't you fink?

Beat.

It all a bit too… wiv everyfing, all got a bit flurryin', all got a bit fuckin' flustery, we gotta, d'you know what I mean?

ROLLY. Yeah.

PINK. This is gonna kick-start da new beginnin', da new horizon.

Beat.

This is da first scamper.

Beat.

But it a marathon not a sprint. 'Member dat.

ROLLY. Why?

PINK. Cos it essential.

Beat.

ROLLY. Where you get it?

PINK. Slimy Steve solt it me. Wanted a fiver, but took four quid in da end. (*Nods at CD player.*) Chucked in a zig machine an' all. Was janglin' like a –

ROLLY. What it for?

PINK. What you mean?

ROLLY. What you do wiv it?

PINK. What?

ROLLY. What da –

PINK. It a juicer.

ROLLY. Yeah…

PINK. It juices shit.

ROLLY. It juices shit?

PINK. Veg an' dat. It juices veg.

ROLLY. What for?

PINK. To drink.

ROLLY. It juices veg to drink. Right.

Silence. They look at the juicer.

PINK. It does fruits an' all.

Beat.

We can conjure some smoothies. Strawberry smoothies. Strawberry an' banana an' blueberry an –

ROLLY. What for?

PINK. To fuckin' drink. Why you fuckin' think?

Beat.

It is healthy. Part of five a day. In Sweden it eleven a day.
Dey must be shittin' for an Olympic Gold, dem blondies.
Eleven a day. It fuckin' unnatural. It –

ROLLY. Why don't we munch da fruits an' veg?

PINK. Cos it easier to gulp it.

Beat.

An' vegetables tasty like shit.

Beat.

We get all our vitaminisation from one glug.

Beat.

ROLLY. What we gonna juice?

PINK *looks round. Finds a half-eaten pizza on a plate. She
opens the juicer, scrapes off the tomato sauce and onions
into the juicer. Looks at the solid result.* PINK *finds a half-
drunk mug of tea. She adds this to the mix. Blitzes it. She
finds a glass and pours the results into a glass. They both
look at it. A long time.*

PINK. We gotta start propellin' forwarding.

Beat.

We gotta take better nurture of ourselves, innit. You gotta take
better cares of you an' da pup. Won't be long now. We gotta
get to a betta place. We can't keep on keepin' on like dis.

Beat.

We done need to create a bomb-proof plan, innit.

Beat.

I decided I gonna be a personal trainer in da gym or somewhere or maybe over da park like doze ones over da park. When we done it, maded da changes an' dat. I's pretty vigorous. Can do dem stairs in da station no bother. All dem fat fucks clammed up an' fixed on da escalator, like dey got all da time in da fuckin' world. I can belt dem steps in a nano.

Beat.

What you gonna do? An' don't spiel 'bout dat hotel.

ROLLY. Dunno.

PINK. What you fink you's good at?

ROLLY. Nuttin.

PINK. Course you are. Everyone's good at somefing.

Beat.

What do you like?

ROLLY. Twixes.

PINK. Apart from Twixes.

ROLLY. Old people.

PINK. Do ya?

ROLLY. Used to love Sylvia, Jayne's mum.

Smell of aftershave. Strong. All pervasive. PINK *smells it. Moves away.*

Used to bring yellow-an'-pink-square cake an' telt me 'bout da old times.

Beat.

Magic ten pence out of my lug.

Beat.

Telt rude ha-ha's.

PINK *quickly puts on the CD, quietly. Smells the air. Puts her hand over her mouth.*

An' brush my tangles.

Beat.

I wanna toil wiv da old ones.

Beat.

Don't needs to be gold star wiv da numbers for dat.

Beat. PINK *sniffs the air. Covers her nose and moves.*

Do you fink dey let me?

Beat.

PINK. Can you smelt dat?

ROLLY. What?

Beat.

PINK. Nuttin.

> PINK *stands near the CD player, hand hovering over the volume.*

ROLLY. Will dey let me toil wiv da old ones?

PINK. Why not?

ROLLY. Cos I been inside –

PINK. Won't matter. No one gives a shit 'bout da old ones.

> *Beat.* PINK *sniffs the air. The smell has disappeared. Gone. She moves away from the CD player.*

ROLLY. Dat's it den, dat's what I's gonna do.

PINK. You should.

ROLLY. Yeah, why not?

PINK. Yeah.

ROLLY. I's gonna go down da Jobbage Centre.

PINK. Why da fuck not?

ROLLY. Find out 'bout toilin' wiv da old ones.

PINK. You go, girl. Girl power.

ROLLY. In a oldie home wiv lots of nice old ones teltin' dem stories.

PINK. And I's gonna be a personal fitness trainer instructoress.

ROLLY. You should.

PINK. Work at Gym Bollocks dot Com.

ROLLY. Why not?

PINK. Get all dem buff men buffer an' da fat slags skinnier.

ROLLY. Why da fuck not?

PINK. Encourage dem. Run, fatty, run. Look, iced bun over dere, chase it, cauliflower arse.

ROLLY. Yeah.

PINK. We ditch da gnaw, yeah? We go full-on clean an' we, both of us, both of us mind, be bleachy, yeah. Wipe clean, minty fresh, da both of us, both of us, yeah?

ROLLY. Yeah, both of us clean, yeah.

PINK. No gnaw, no juice –

ROLLY. No nuttin.

PINK. We imbibe dem veg smoothies, an' I'll get meself some Lycra an' a sports bra from Sports Direct an' we get dem jobs.

ROLLY. Yeah, me wiv da olds an' you –

PINK. We toil mental hard an' we wins da gold star for best toiler. We feels satisfication an' all good cos we earned our monies an' never crimed for it.

ROLLY. No, we never.

PINK. An' when it our holidays, our work holidays, our four weeks off, we go Galapagos. Cos we deserve it. Galapagos. Amazing fuckin' wildlife. Swimmin' lizards an' everyfing. Incredible swimmin' lizards dat eat da seaweed an' –

ROLLY. Swimmin' lizards dat eat da seaweed.

PINK. Yeah. Magic, innit. And why shouldn't we? Why
shouldn't we go dere? We work fuckin' hard. We deserving
of our four weeks. Tons of peoples go holidaying. An' not
just to some shit campsite wiv other pups in care. Not just
some windy fuckhole wiv orange tents an' pervs trying to
look at your tit-tats. (*Beat.*) We could go back to Camber
Sands. D'ya 'member Camber Sands?

ROLLY. Yeah, Camber Sands, innit.

PINK. Fuckin' beautiful. All dat sand. Beautifulness. Was
fuckin' brilliant, 'member? You 'member?

Sound of laughter, sound of the sea.

Dat's when we first lugged da song. In dat caravan. We kept
rotatin' it an' rotatin' it. An' Dad chucked it in da sand dunes
cos we trilled it all da time an' it done got on his tits.

(*Sings.*) I'd while away da hours –

ROLLY (*joins in*). Conferrin' wiv da flowers –

PINK *and* ROLLY. Consultin' wiv da rain.

Beat.

PINK. You must have done been 'bout seven, eight. Maybe
seven. I was eleven. I 'member cos my bleeds started. I
'member in da middle of da night, diggin' a hole on da beach
an' sittin' down. Feelin' so fuckin'… Lookin' up at da
moon… feelin' so fuckin… like… like I was da earth an' da
earth was all me. Dat we was all meshed up. Lookin' down
an' dere a pool of blood dat was me. In da sand. It was me.
An' da sea came in an' tooked da blood away, washed it out
an' I thinked I am part of dis world. I am part of dis. I am
part of dis world.

ROLLY. Yeah, part of dis world.

PINK. An' we sleeped out on da beach. We dragged our blankie
on da sand an' snoozed an' eyeballed up at da stars an' it was
beautifulness an' I done cuddle you all up to keep you warm

an' snuggery an' you loved it an' we could trill as loud as we want an' we wake up wiv all sand in our hair an' lugs an' stuff an' salt in our lashes an' our teefs all icy and our toes all blue an' we laugh an' we laugh an' we laugh an' we laugh an' we –

ROLLY. We could boat over to France.

Beat.

Jayne an' Mike tooked me to France, dat first summer.

PINK. What 'bout New York?

Beat.

We could fly New York, innit.

Beat.

New York? Yeah. New York. Dat's it. Dat's de one. We should 'totally like totally like totally go to Nu Yawk'. Seed da Twin Towers an' dat, seed dat hole. Go to Central Perk. Yeah, man. New fuckin' York –

There's a knock at the door. PINK *gets up, still talking.*

Why not? Why fuckin' not? Save up da work monies. Treat ourselfs. We deserving of it. Go on da Sex an' da City tour an' we should eyeball LA while we dere. Yeah. A roady trip. A fuckin' roady trip. It be amazin'. It be –

PINK *opens the door. Outside is a* WOMAN *dressed in jeans and a floral top – non-threatening. A beat.* PINK *slams the door shut. The* WOMAN's *foot jams in the doorway.* PINK *tries to kick it away. The* WOMAN *perseveres. She pushes the door open.* PINK *backs away.* ROLLY *looks for an exit. There isn't one.* PINK *goes to the CD player and turns the music right up, top volume.* ROLLY *stands in the corner of the room. She bares her teeth at the* WOMAN. *With calm and reassuring presence, the* WOMAN *approaches* ROLLY. *When she reaches her, she stops. She takes a blanket from her bag and puts it over her shoulder. She unzips the front of* ROLLY's *tracksuit. She pulls out a fully formed baby-sized rat from* ROLLY's *womb and gently*

wraps the blanket round it. She holds it against her chest.
ROLLY *stands dead still.* PINK *watches. The* WOMAN
does up the zip on ROLLY's *tracksuit and quietly and*
unobtrusively moves away. She pulls the door gently behind
her. Silence. ROLLY *holds her belly. Agony.* PINK *turns*
away. The music plays on.

Scene Eight

ROLLY *sits in the corner of the room, wasted.* PINK *is*
bouncing off the walls.

PINK. I's on me toes, man. On me toes. I telt him, don't touch
me. Take dem paws off me, man. 'S what I telt, innit. He
withdrewed his paws an' I nutted him. I nutted him proper in
da face. Fell over, claret all over his mush. Runnin' all down.
Gloop an' shit runnin' down his mush. Rushin'. Stuck in his
eyebrow. Pop. Dat's how it went. Pop... Just like – (*Beat.*)
Just like ragin'. Like I was ragin'. Telt him. If he ever did dat
again, I knife him. Knock him out. Splice him. End him.
Fuckin' end him. Tryin' it. (*Beat.*) It was a deal. A fuckin'
done deal. I let you fuck me. You give me da twenty. Ain't
nuttin complicated 'bout it. Do you know what he telt,
fuckin' dirty bastard? Fuckin' ugly greasy tool. He telt. He
telt... 'I thought it was a bogof. Buy one, get one free.' He
thought a fuck would get him a free suck. I telt, 'What do
you think this is?' I telt. 'I ain't Tesco. I ain't fuckin' Tesco. I
don't offer no loyalty points. My cunt ain't trademarked. It
ain't Tesco or Asda or Morrisons or even fuckin' M&S.
"This is not just an ordinary cunt, it an M&S cunt." Nah, it
ain't. My cunt is independent. It is an independent outlet. I
am not a chain. My body is not part of no chain. I am not
situated in a retail park.' He telt, 'You are actually.' An' I
eyeballed round, an' I was. Never realised. Was outside TK
Maxx. Seed these shoes. Winkin' at me. Seed these fuckin'
unbelievable red rouge shimmy shoes. Thinked 'Rolly

should have dem on her foots. Dey would be aces on my
sister Rolly.' Thinked 'Gotta get dem, gotta get Rolly dem
shoes, dem shoes shimmying an' winkin' out at me, teltin'
me, teltin' me zig-a-zig-ah, signage, zig-a-zig-ah, need to get
dem glittery shimmy shoes.' Dat's when he grabbed me. He
grabbed me right on da tit. Hard, pinched me. Nutted him.
Felted fuckin' brilliant. Felted fuckin' yeah. Yeah. Crunched
my foot on his facebones. Screamin' like a fuckin' baby.
Kicked him in da cunt. He all, 'Please. Nah.' Tooked his
wallet. Portrait of his missus an' two pups, one of dem in a,
like, a graduation dress ting an' one of dem 'versity hats. Telt
to him, 'You must be proper puffed up.' An' den I telt him,
'Gonna go round your 'ouse, gonna sit down on your DFS
an' have a cup of Yorkshire wiv your wife an' munch
McVitie's an' wave hi to your pups an' den gonna telt 'em
dat you's a dirty fuckin' bastard.' An' he starts bubblin' up.
All this way an' dat. An' he make me puke. He make me feel
like... I wanna fuckin' kill him. 'Stop tearin', I telt. 'Stop
fuckin' tearin', you baby, you fuckin' pussy baby.' An' he telt
I can have everyfing he got an' he gived me all da greens an'
his watch an all. 'Ta,' I telt him, 'Ta very muchness.'

PINK *hands* ROLLY *a plastic bag. It sits in* ROLLY's *lap.*
ROLLY *makes no attempt to look in it.* PINK *picks it up and*
opens it for her. She takes out a shoebox and puts it on
ROLLY's *lap.* ROLLY *doesn't move.* PINK *picks up the*
shoebox and opens it. She takes out a pair of red glittery
Dorothy-type shoes.

Just right, ain't dey? Just perfection for you.

ROLLY *looks up at her.* PINK *shows her the shoes. No*
reaction. PINK *gets down and puts them on* ROLLY's *feet.*
ROLLY *stares at her feet.*

D'ya love 'em?

Beat.

Keep you all good.

Beat.

Protect ya.

Beat.

Buffer ya. Dey telt me.

Beat.

Cos the 'zig-a-zig-ah' all out now.

Beat.

Dem shoes gonna keep you all cushioned an' treasured an' warm.

Beat.

Promise.

Beat.

Click dem heels together.

Beat.

Click 'em.

PINK *gets down on the floor and clicks* ROLLY*'s feet together*.

Click 'em on your lonesome.

ROLLY *feebly clicks them*.

Dere ain't no place like home.

Beat.

Speak it.

Beat.

Dere ain't no place like home.

Beat.

Speak it.

Beat.

ROLLY. Dere ain't no place like home.

Beat.

PINK. Click an' speak it.

Beat.

ROLLY *clicks her heels together.*

ROLLY. Dere ain't no place like home.

She looks up at PINK. PINK *smiles at her.*

Scene Nine

ROLLY *searching through everything, frantically looking for a wrap of heroin, upturning everything in her path. Chaos.* PINK *sitting very still on the sofa, smoking.* ROLLY *is wearing her red shimmy shoes.* PINK *stares straight ahead.*

Faint white noise interlaced with the low rumble of a male voice – words indecipherable.

ROLLY. I lefted it

Beat.

Hidded it.

Beat.

Definitely.

Beat.

In a safey place.

Beat.

For 'mergencies.

Beat.

I definitely done stashed it –

Beat.

Gimme a paw searchbeamin', gimme a –

Beat.

Split it wiv ya.

Beat.

I for sure put it –

Beat.

It here last –

Beat.

But I –

Beat.

I –

Beat.

Yeah.

Beat.

Fuck.

Beat.

My bones…

Beat.

Fuck.

Beat.

Was here.

Beat.

Knowed it was.

Beat.

You seed it?

Beat.

Was a hundred per cent –

Beat.

You's alright, innit. You's –

Beat.

Done you –

Beat.

You tooked it, innit.

Beat.

You tiefed my –

Beat.

Cos you –

Beat.

Wiv my –

Beat.

Can't done find it cos you –

Beat.

You stolt it.

Beat.

You fuckin' tiefed –

Beat.

And tucked it.

Beat.

Yeah…

Beat.

You scurried it off an' –

Beat.

Shot it.

Beat.

Bitch.

Beat.

Fuckin' bitch.

ROLLY *stares defiantly at* PINK *and kicks off her red shimmy shoes.*

A man's laughter, footsteps on the stairs.

PINK *turns to look at* ROLLY. *Sees her shoes are off.* PINK *quickly gets up.*

Gimme my fuckin' –

Beat.

Gimme –

Beat.

Whatever crumbs you done got left.

PINK *forces the shoes back on to* ROLLY*'s feet.*

Laughter and footsteps cease. White noise continues.

You's alright, ain't ya?

Beat.

Sorted your own veins out, yeah?

Beat.

Gold star for you, gold star for fuckin' you.

Beat.

I spread it out, share around.

Beat.

Please, I'm lousyfied, I'm –

Beat.

Gimme some of –

Beat.

Fuckin' selfish cunt.

Beat.

Everyone know it.

Beat.

Everyone's always knowed it.

Beat.

Forever done do what you wants.

Beat.

Like when you kilt my bird.

Beat.

At Jayne an' Mike's.

Beat.

When I happened on da baby hurted sparrow bird an' I was mendin' it tiptop, because it was a poorly chap.

Beat.

An' den you come round an' completed it.

Beat.

You ordered me closed up my eyeballs, count to ten an' squeezed at it as fierced as I could.

Beat.

Dem little soft bones all broked an' da warm wet stuff slip through an' when I opened up, claret on da carpet an' poorly chap sparrow all squozen up in my paws.

Beat.

You telt Jayne dat we let it fly to freedom cos it all restored.

Silence. No response from PINK. ROLLY *moves to her and stands in front of her. She slowly and deliberately lifts her feet up and begins to take the shoes off again.*

Footsteps approaching. Tap-tap on the door. Tap-tap on the door.

PINK *quickly gets up again. She goes to a drawer and takes out some parcel tape.*

PINK *stands in front of* ROLLY, *eye to eye.*

PINK. I let Red-eyed Paul an' his stinkin' mate Twitchy McDonald fuck me up da arse, mouth an' cunt every night for a month to pay off your damage.

Beat.

When dey came searchlightin' for all da greens you owed. I never had it so I gaved da only thing I had.

She gets down on the floor and she tapes the shoes to ROLLY'*s feet.* ROLLY *lets her.* PINK *stands back and looks at* ROLLY'*s feet. She looks at* ROLLY. *Beat.* ROLLY *turns away.*

ROLLY. I knowed it was here.

Beat.

Lefted it.

Beat.

You tooked it.

Beat.

I knowed I lefted it –

Beat.

I did, I fuckin' –

Beat.

I's sick.

Beat.

Fuckin' cluckin'.

Beat.

Please.

Beat.

I knowed I tucked it some –

Beat.

For 'mergencies.

Scene Ten

PINK *is alone. She sits on the floor. The walls are covered with an ever-increasing conversation. She sits looking at the words.*

I miss you

I miss you too

I come to you to your nest

Is that what you want?

That's what I want

I miss you

She a cunt

Yeah

She a cunt She a wretched fucking cunt-faced hag She a dirty lying faced shit stink ball She a rotter a piece of shit Vileness of the highest order I never wanted to live wiv her I never wanted to be wiv her.

I know.

I wish you was my sister.

Do you?

Yes.

I miss you.

She a dirty beast a red-faced black-souled nasty stupid head.
She killed the poorly chap.

Yes.

I wish I could turn her insides out I wish I could splitted her
from eye to foots To pull all the red stuff to pull out all the
bloods and the guts and the shits and the yellows.

Yes.

I leave this foulness this stink this cancer pit.

I miss you.

I wish you was my sister.

Do you?

I'm gonna take off the red rouge No Place Like Home
shimmy shoes and never gonna wear them ever again I
miss you.

I miss you too.

Protectin' us. Ha. Ha. Ha. Ha.

What from?

Keepin' us safe. Ha. Ha. Ha. Ha. Ha. Ha.

What from?

Ha. Ha. Ha. Ha. Ha. Ha. Ha.

PINK *stands up halfway through reading, goes to the drawer
and pulls out the tape. She picks up newspaper and tries to
stick it over the writing. It is impossible. Every time she tries,
the writing re-emerges. She tries to cover it. She throws the*

paper on the floor. She tries to cover the words with her body, her hands, but they run over her, flowing over her body, flowing over her face.

Ha. Ha. Ha. Ha. Ha. Ha. Ha. Ha.

She closes her eyes.

Ha. Ha. Ha. Ha. Ha. Ha. Ha. Ha.

Scene Eleven

PINK *faces* ROLLY. ROLLY*'s clothes are ripped. Face bleeding. No shoes on.*

ROLLY. It ain't my fault. I was lyin' dere. Dey just stoled 'em. Tugged 'em off my foots. I's right sorrowed, but... It weren't my fault. I couldn't done do nuttin. Dey just powered over. Right over, gotted in my face. Couldn't see proper, but dere was hordes of da buggers, was conquered by dem all, all of dem all roar an' roar an' roar. Wanted dem shimmy shoes. Wanted dem so bad. Love dem shimmy shoes. Alright, alright, it was just one. Dey was one. She camed over when I was heaped on da floor. She scampered over, da girl, an' she collected her moment an' tugged 'em. Cos I was all bleurgh an' flopped an' couldn't move none. She tugged 'em an' legged it. I eyeballed her go off on those wheelie shoes, dem shoes wiv da wheels. She wheelied off. She tugged da red shimmies an' she wheelied off, before I could – I know what you ponderin' – how could I let a little girl ting tief my shoes? How could dat happened? To dem shimmy, red rouge There No Place Like Home shoes? She weren't even no big girl. She a liccle one. Not a growed-up small one, not a Lilliputian, not a Oompa Loompa. But a proper little one, plaits an' beads an' shiny backpack. Don't be angryfied on me, it weren't my fault. I's on da floor. I's all crunched on da pavement, face in da glass. Da bruise man boot me out his

car. He pulled my fur, caught my whiskers, gobbed green at
me, punched me in da schnoze an' booted me out. Dat little
beady wiv da wheels eyed me on da pavement an' dat's when
she tugged 'em. I hitted my head on da kerb. Had da wobbles.
Was all… Had da wobbles. He was a right ugly skull, eyes
dat went all criss-cross, all everywhere, north, south, east,
west. Gonna telt Stitch an' Black Rush to seek him out, innit.
I never did nuttin. I'll go get more of dem shoes. Never you
be bothered. Never you… Where did you get 'em? Surprised
she could spot 'em, she had dem thick glasses on, little tief.
She had dem wizard glasses. Da boy wizard. Da Dumbledore
an' da muggles. Dem glasses. Iccle shoe tief in Harry Potter
spaz glasses. Fuckin' four-eyed spaz little tief wheelie cunt
took dem shimmy No Place Like Home shoes.

The blade of a knife appears through the wall.

He never paid up neither. I's gonna call it all over, already
seen four cash-dicks befores him, but den he droved up in his
jumbo car an' I thinked, 'Here come da greens.' Wearing a
suit an' speakin' all la-di-da Downton. I thinked, 'He see me
an' Pink alright for time, get it all in, get us stocked up an'
dat, get us crammed, our bloods cooled an' our heads
soothed.' Fucked me, spatted at me, punched me an' kicked
me. Den gave me fuck-all. Fuck-all.

Another blade appears.

Speaked I's lucky he done dint have his weaponry on him.

Beat.

Telt he usually has a machete in dat jumbo car.

And another.

Never even pay me my winnings.

Beat.

I took his spunk up my ting an' all. Telt he'd pay da extra.

PINK *gets up.*

Never even done pay me da basic, da Tesco basic.

PINK *goes to the front door.*

Never gaved me a bean.

Beat.

Not a bean.

PINK *goes out.*

Not a fuckin' bean.

Scene Twelve

ROLLY *lying on the floor, wasted.* PINK, *now wearing the red shimmy shoes, pulls the needle from her neck. A moment of ecstasy. She crumples onto the sofa. Her eyes close. Both wasted.* PINK *smiles. A long time.* PINK *looks over at* ROLLY. *She reaches for her hand. They hold hands. A long time.*

Sun shines, seagulls fly, a kite floats by, children giggle, waves shimmer.

PINK. Rolly?

Beat.

ROLLY. Yeah?

Beat.

PINK. It don't get better dan dis, eh?

Beat.

ROLLY. Yeah.

Beat.

PINK. MasterChef, innit.

Beat.

ROLLY. Yeah.

Beat.

PINK. It don't get better dan dis.

Beat.

ROLLY. Yeah.

Beat.

PINK. Greg Torode, innit.

Beat.

ROLLY. Yeah.

Beat.

PINK. Yeah.

Beat.

ROLLY. Yeah

Beat.

PINK. Yeah.

Beat.

ROLLY. Yeah.

Beat.

PINK. It don't get better dan dis.

Beat.

I loves you.

Beat.

ROLLY. I loves you too, May.

Scene Thirteen

PINK *alone. A* MAN *stands on the edge of room.* PINK *has two mini Mars bars in her hand. She looks at them. The* MAN *watches her. She looks at him. Silence.*

PINK. Hello.

Scene Fourteen

PINK *takes a load of sat-navs out of her tracksuit.* ROLLY *sits in the nest.*

PINK. A massive fuckin' alarm screeched out wiv dis last one. Da owner came leggin' out like a B52 an' dis tiny iccle woof under his arm.

Beat.

Comes leggin' it in his jimi-jams, silly fuckin' feathercap, all flappin' 'bout. Him in his jimi-jams. Nearly fuckin' chuckled. Don't know what his problem is. He be insured, innit. All dem cunts up Broadywalk got da insurance in dem fourbefour battleships anyways. Daftie fuckin' chomps, runnin' out in his jimi-jams. I could've been a danger, could've had a blade. Could've sliced his face. Sliced his face an' kilt his dog.

ROLLY. I speaked to May.

PINK. What?

ROLLY. I speaked to May.

PINK. When?

ROLLY. Yesterdays.

Beat.

I speaked to her.

Beat.

I runged her from a different number.

Beat.

She put da beep down as soon as she hearded done telt it was me.

Beat.

So I runged again.

Beat.

An' I kept an' kept tilt she answered.

Beat.

I kept an' kepted.

Beat.

I kept an' kepted tilt she speaked to me.

PINK *goes to a bag and unzips it. She starts putting all the sat-navs in the bag.*

PINK. Dese see us all gold star for time –

ROLLY. She was crammed full of da tremble –

PINK (*ignoring*). Spice up da bloods for a bit –

ROLLY. Telt she couldn't ain't speak to me –

PINK (*ignoring*). Keep us away from dem fuckin' cash-dicks –

ROLLY. Telt a big bruise man scuttled over her flat –

PINK (*ignoring*). I got da itch –

ROLLY. Day after da interview at da hotel –

PINK (*ignoring*). Got da inbetween-legs itch –

ROLLY. Tolt her not to speaked to me –

PINK (*ignoring*). We can nest here, all safey, warm an' –

ROLLY. Telt her if she speaked to me, he kill her pup.

Beat. PINK *stands up, shoves her hands in her pockets. She feels something. She pulls out her hands and looks at one of them. She slowly opens her hand, a handful of shiny pound coins sit in her palm. She stares at them.*

Why someone do dat?

Beat.

Telt her dat he kilt her pup if she speaked to me.

Beat.

Telt May dat?

Beat.

What was da bruise man like, I arksed –

Beat.

Had a scar across his gullet she telt –

Beat.

Why done Slo Mo go to May an' telt her he kilt her pup?

PINK *shoves her other hand in her other pocket. Slowly she pulls out another handful of shiny pound coins. She stares at both hands.*

Why done did you telt him to do dat?

Beat.

Why did you done do dat?

PINK *quickly goes to the bag and throws the coins in. She zips it up and moves away.*

Why?

Beat.

Why?

PINK. Why did you nest wiv Jayne an' Mike?

ROLLY. What?

PINK. Why did you go nest wiv dem?

ROLLY. Dat is not –

PINK. Why did you nest wiv Jayne an' Mike?

ROLLY. Dunno why you –

PINK. Why did –

ROLLY. I was a little 'un

PINK. I was a little 'un.

ROLLY. You was twelve.

PINK. Yeah, a little 'un.

ROLLY. Why did you telt –

PINK. It all equal now.

Beat.

You wanted to live wiv Jayne an' Mike an' you did. I wanted to live wiv Jayne an' Mike an' I didn't. You wanted to live wiv May an' you didn't. I didn't want you to live wiv May an' you didn't. Equal. Adds up. All's fair. No winners. Just sames.

Beat.

ROLLY. You telt me good for youse 'bout da hotel an' interview. Good for youse an' good lucks.

PINK *sees a heap of shiny pound coins on the side. She stops.*

PINK. Why dey never wanted me?

ROLLY. That's whatted you telt me.

Beat.

You waved me off full of da luck an' da wishes.

PINK. Why dey never –

ROLLY. Fingers crossed an' –

PINK. Could have tooked da both of us.

ROLLY. Rah rah rah.

PINK. Tooked da both. No bother.

ROLLY. May was trembled.

PINK. I was trembled.

ROLLY. She was –

PINK. I was.

   Beat.

ROLLY. You should ain't never should have –

PINK. You should ain't never –

ROLLY. I never did nuttin.

PINK. Dey could've done placed me an' all. Jayne an' Mike –

ROLLY. Dey never have da area, dey couldn't –

PINK. Dey could have –

ROLLY. Dey couldn't ain't squozed you in.

PINK. Jayne never inclined to me.

ROLLY. Dat ain't –

PINK. Cos she green.

ROLLY. What?

PINK. She green as –

ROLLY. Why would she be –

PINK. Cos of Mike.

   Beat.

ROLLY. What 'bout Mike?

PINK. You knows.

ROLLY. I don't.

PINK. You do, you right proper sewed-up do.

ROLLY. Nah.

PINK. As if.

ROLLY. I dunno what ya –

PINK. What you pretendy for?

ROLLY. I ain't.

PINK. Cos of da fuckin'.

Pause.

ROLLY. What?

Beat.

PINK. He was fuckin' me.

Beat.

Mike. Jayne's Mike was –

ROLLY. Dat ain't truthfulness.

PINK. It is.

ROLLY. Why you mouthed dat?

PINK. Cos it factuality.

ROLLY. It ain't.

PINK. It is.

Beat.

When you was downstairs eyeballin' da Christmas goggle-box.

Beat.

When you was openin' your fizzbomb birthday pressies.

ROLLY. I ain't believin' you.

Pause.

Mike was a kindly one.

PINK. You fink so?

ROLLY. He weren't like –

PINK. He was.

ROLLY. Mike was a good man.

PINK. None of da mans is good.

Beat.

ROLLY. Mike was gold star. I done knowed he was.

PINK. Dat's why she ain't never wanted me 'round.

Beat.

Only Christmas an' birthdays cos –

ROLLY. No.

PINK. She was green.

ROLLY. She weren't green.

PINK. She pea-green fuckin' bitch who couldn't keep her man –

ROLLY. Nah, she –

PINK. Couldn't keep her pervert fuckin' husband paedo's paws
off of me –

ROLLY. Dat wasn't –

PINK. Let him fuck me –

ROLLY. Nah.

PINK. Let him tear me wide, let him –

ROLLY. Nah.

PINK. Get inside me wiv his –

ROLLY. Nah.

PINK. Push up on me, this way, dat –

ROLLY. Nah.

PINK. Push his claws in my –

ROLLY. Shut up.

PINK. Scratch me, hold me down, bite me –

ROLLY. Shut da fuck up.

PINK. Scrape my fur –

ROLLY. She did want you dere.

PINK. Stretch me till I bleeds.

ROLLY. Jayne did want you.

PINK. Stretch me till I bubble.

ROLLY. She did.

PINK. Cram a sock on my mouth to stop da whimper.

ROLLY. She arksed me.

Beat.

She arksed me if you should come an' live wiv us. She
arksed me what I thinked. She satted me down an' she
questioned, 'What would you thinked 'bout your sista comin'
to live here wiv us? How would you feeled? Be honest.'
(*Beat.*) Mike wasn't like dat. He was a gold star, I knowed he
was. He was a smiley face an' a tick on da chart. He –

PINK. What did you telt her?

Beat.

When she arksed you?

ROLLY. I telt her yes.

Beat.

I telt her dat I yearned for you to –

Beat.

I telt her wiv all my beatin' heart dat I –

PINK. Wiv all your beatin' heart?

ROLLY. Dat you must come. Come nest with me an' Jayne an'
    Mike. Dat I would bubble every day if you never ain't come
    an' nest with us. Together. Me an' my sister Pink nestin'
    together with Jayne an' Mike an' me. Rolly an' Pink an'
    Jayne an' Mike an' Happy Ever Afters.

Pause.

PINK. Swear.

ROLLY. Swear.

PINK. Swear on your life.

ROLLY. Swear on my life.

PINK. Swear on my life.

ROLLY. Swear on your life.

PINK. Swear on your pup's life.

Beat.

Swear on your baby's life.

ROLLY *looks away. Silence.*

ROLLY. Jayne an' Mike, dey maded me feel…

Beat.

Round dem I feeled…

Beat.

Clean. Bleach clean.

Silence.

Did Mike ever –

PINK. Nah.

ROLLY. Truth?

PINK. He done never polluted nuttin. Was a gold star.

Scene Fifteen

PINK *alone. Two* MEN *stand on the edge of the room, watching her. She looks at them. She is wearing her red shimmy shoes and holding a teddy bear.*

PINK. Thank you.

Scene Sixteen

PINK *is lying down, wasted.* ROLLY *sits far away from her. Silence.*

PINK. Rolly?

>   *Pause.*

>   Sista?

>   *Pause.*

>   You dere?

>   *Pause.*

>   Rolly?

>   *Pause.*

>   You dere?

>   *Beat.*

>   Is you…

ROLLY. Yeah.

>   *Beat.*

PINK. Good.

>   *Beat.*

ROLLY. Yeah.

>   *Beat.*

PINK. Gold star.

> ROLLY *mouths the words 'gold star' at the same time.*

> *Silence.*

> Rolly?

> *Pause.*

> Rolly?

> *Pause.*

> You dere?

ROLLY. Yeah.

PINK. Good.

> *Beat.*

> Gold star.

> ROLLY *mouths the words 'gold star' at the same time.*

> *Silence.*

> Rolly?

ROLLY. Yeah.

PINK. Sista?

ROLLY. Yeah.

PINK. You dere?

ROLLY. Yeah.

PINK. Good.

ROLLY. Yeah.

Scene Seventeen

PINK *sits waiting on the sofa.*

White noise, crackling, growling.

PINK. Where da fuck you been –

> *Beat.*

> I is fuckin' –

> *Beat.*

> You telt you be minutes.

ROLLY. Bumped into Slo Mo an'–

PINK. Don't give a fuck.

ROLLY. Got chattin' –

PINK. Don't give a fuckage.

ROLLY. Ain't seed dem for time –

PINK. I's fuckin –

ROLLY. An' den I was scurryin' from da stinkin holes –

PINK. I's janglin'.

ROLLY. I seed dis.

PINK. Give me da fuckin' –

ROLLY. Dis is what I seed.

> ROLLY *gets out a piece of paper from her jacket. She unfolds it and holds it up to.*

PINK. Where de –

ROLLY. Scrutinise.

PINK. Gimme the –

ROLLY. Open dem eyeballs an' scrutinise.

> PINK *takes the paper and looks at it. She hands it back to* ROLLY. ROLLY *doesn't take it.*

PINK. Where the –

ROLLY. Ain't smiley face, is it?

PINK. Gimme the –

ROLLY. Ain't gold –

PINK. Gimme the –

ROLLY. Read it out.

PINK. Gimme da gnaw.

ROLLY. Read it.

PINK. Gimme da fuckin' –

ROLLY shows her the wraps. PINK goes to grab at them. ROLLY moves off.

ROLLY. I give you whence you readed it.

Beat.

Whence you.

Beat.

G'on.

Beat.

PINK (*reads*). Serious assault.

Beat.

Can you help?

Pause.

ROLLY. Finish.

Beat.

All of it.

PINK (*reading*). At 'bout 9.30 on Thursday 27th September a young girl of eight years was seriously assaulted on Shelton Parade.

Pause. ROLLY *motions for* PINK *to read it.* PINK *doesn't.* ROLLY *takes it from her and reads it to her.*

ROLLY (*reading, childlike, halting*). The attacker is described as female, white, five feet, slim build, blonde hair. Do you recognise the description of this woman? (*Pause, hands it back.*) Finish.

PINK *snatches it from her.*

PINK (*reading quickly*). Were you in or near Shelton Parade, Gosport Lane, Arnold Street around this time? Did you see the incident or anythin' dat could help. Please contact blah blah pigs at the station. (*Hands back the poster.*) Now, gimme.

Beat.

ROLLY. You done battered dat iccle girl.

Beat.

You battered da iccle shoe tief in Harry Potter spaz glasses.

Beat.

You losted her her eyeball.

Beat.

You battered her so hard she losted her fuckin' eyeball.

Beat.

All over dem shimmy shoes.

Beat.

Dem fuckin' red rouge shimmy No Place Like Home shoes.

PINK. Gimme my –

ROLLY. Why you done dat?

PINK. You telt you'd –

ROLLY. Why?

PINK. Gimme –

ROLLY. When you telt me why you –

PINK. Wouldn't surrender dem.

ROLLY. How could you done dat?

PINK. She all swearin' an' wheelin' off –

ROLLY. How could you done batter dat –

PINK. Arksed her nice as pie –

ROLLY. Iccle speccy wheelie girl –

PINK. I arks her, but she weren't surrendin', so I –

ROLLY. Punched her iccle face in.

Beat.

Smashed her Harry Potter spaz glasses into her eyeballs.

PINK. Dey was comin'.

ROLLY. Blooded an' broked one of dem.

PINK. Dey was comin'.

ROLLY. Broked one of her eyeballs.

Beat.

PINK. Dey was comin'.

Beat.

ROLLY. Dey wasn't.

PINK. Dey was. Dey is –

ROLLY. Dey ain't.

PINK. Dey is. Please gimme the –

ROLLY. It all clouded in your bonce again. It all in your fuckin' crazed-up –

PINK. Gimme my –

ROLLY. She da same age as your Tia, you know dat?

ROLLY. Just gimme –

ROLLY. How you feeled if you heard telt someone done dat to Tia.

PINK. I's warnin' you –

ROLLY. If your Tia went back to her Jayne an' Mike's or her whoever's –

PINK. I's fuckin' warnin' you, just –

ROLLY. All dirtied up an' bubblin' –

PINK. She tiefed dem.

ROLLY. All scareded an' hurted.

PINK. She tiefed dem shimmy –

ROLLY. With claret poured out of her socket.

PINK. Gimme my –

ROLLY. All gunge an' red an' shards smashed up in her iccle girl sweet skin.

PINK. You is so fuckin' –

ROLLY. Yeah?

PINK. I gonna fuckin' –

ROLLY. Is you?

PINK. Gimme the –

> PINK *launches herself at* ROLLY. ROLLY *kicks her off.* PINK *hits the floor hard. A beat.* ROLLY *pulls the shoes from* PINK*'s feet and holds them up in front of her. White noise intensifies, cars pulling up, car doors slammed, a doorbell, low murmer of male voices.*

> Please.

> *Beat.*

ROLLY. Nah.

> *Beat.*

PINK. Please.

ROLLY (*holds up the wraps and the shoes*). Which?

PINK. Please, my bones –

   Beat.

   My bonce –

   Beat.

ROLLY. Which?

PINK. Dem shoes, dem –

ROLLY. Why?

   Pause.

   Dey ain't bufferin' you.

PINK. Gimme my –

ROLLY. Dey ain't doin' nuttin.

PINK. I need my –

ROLLY. Dey just shoes.

PINK. Dey ain't. Dey –

ROLLY. Dey just fuckin' shoes.

PINK. Protect us.

   Beat.

   Keep you wiv me.

ROLLY. What?

PINK. Dem shimmy red rouge No Place Like Home shoes keeped you here.

ROLLY. Nah.

PINK. Safe with me.

ROLLY. Nah.

PINK. Keeped you tended an' warm an' all here.

ROLLY. Nah.

PINK. Wiv me. Hold you here in da snuggery.

Beat.

ROLLY. You done dat.

Beat.

Keeped me here.

PINK. Keeped us all –

ROLLY. You done it.

Beat.

You done gettin' in da way of all of everyfing.

Beat.

Gettin' in da way of me gettin' it all straight an' proper an' right.

Beat.

Fuckin' it up for me an' May.

PINK. We equal now. We all da sames.

ROLLY. We ain't equal.

PINK. No winner, no losers, both same.

ROLLY. You da winner.

PINK. No, I –

ROLLY. You fuck it upped for me at dat Downton hotel.

PINK. No, I –

ROLLY. Yeah, Slo Mo telt me what you maded him to do.

PINK. I –

ROLLY. He telt me all 'bout it.

PINK. Cos I afeared for you. Look like bad place.

ROLLY. Telt me dat you –

PINK. Cos I afeared.

ROLLY. Crumpled it for me.

PINK. Cos I –

ROLLY. Fuck it all upped.

PINK. Better like dis.

ROLLY. Fuck it upped for me an' May.

PINK. We safe.

ROLLY. Fuck it upped for me an' Jayne an' Mike.

PINK. Together, we –

ROLLY. Makin' dem hate on me.

PINK. It just us now.

ROLLY. Keepin' me all close.

PINK. It gotta be only us.

ROLLY. Stockaded me here.

PINK. Me an' you.

ROLLY. Ruin everyfing.

PINK. Us two iccle ones –

ROLLY. Makin' –

PINK. Together in our nest.

ROLLY. Makin' me –

PINK. Lookin' up in da sky.

ROLLY. Makin' me grip –

PINK. Up at da blue black sky.

ROLLY. Makin' me grip on –

PINK. Up at da twinkle stars and da moon.

ROLLY. Makin' me grip on youse.

ROLLY *moves to get her phone. It is by the spot. She looks at it. Silence.*

PINK. Rolly, I –

ROLLY. I dun this project inside, could click pictures of whatever we wanted. May telt me to click things dat make me wanna gnaw, everyfing dat make me wanna fill up my veins an' forget. Telted she wanted to understand. (*Beat.*) She ain't never taken nuttin in her life.

Beat.

'Magine dat.

Beat.

'Magine not wantin' to.

Pause.

I clicked my cell, a roast dinner, da outside walkin' place, a nasty screw, a nice one, da blue sky, da grey sky, da sun, da grass, a pigeon, some stars, da bars, da door, my teeth, my fingers, my veins, da lock, a spill on da floor, an old one on my wing an' my toothbrush.

Beat.

May done looked at mine pictures an' she bubbled up dese great big tears.

Silence.

You lefted dat gnaw out, purpose like, didn't you?

Beat.

By da spot.

Beat.

By da beep.

Beat.

You lefted a wrap full –

PINK. I never –

ROLLY. You knowed I wouldn't ain't ever be able to –

PINK. Nah, dat ain't –

ROLLY. You knowed.

PINK. I never, I –

ROLLY. You done knowed I could never combat it.

PINK. It was accident. I –

ROLLY. No one ain't never splashed tears 'bout me before.

PINK. I have.

ROLLY. Nah.

PINK. I have, when you was –

ROLLY. Nah, you always teared 'bout yourself.

> ROLLY *starts gathering her stuff together. She starts to pull the few belongs she has into a bag. White noise intensifies. Low rumble of male voices, laughter, footsteps on the stairs.*

PINK. Please.

> *Beat.*

Please.

> *Beat.*

Bad tings will…

> *Beat.*

Please.

> *Tap-tap on the door.*

Dey comin'.

> *Tap-tap on the door.*

> ROLLY *puts the shoes on the table.*

Please.

The door opens.

Please, don't.

ROLLY *puts the wraps of heroin down on the table by the shoes.*

Please.

Keys thrown on the dresser. Tap-tap on the door.

Dey is all comin'.

Footsteps on the stairs. Tap-tap on the door.

Dey is all comin' for me.

The door opens.

ROLLY *goes to the front door.*

ROLLY. Put dem shimmy shoes on den. Keep ya right.

ROLLY *opens the door and goes out.*

A smell of aftershave. The MEN *arrive.* PINK *looks at them all, in turn. They all stand round the edge of the room. They watch impassively. She takes out a packet of cigarettes, Silk Cut, looks at the pack, takes one out and lights it. She looks at the* MEN, *each one in turn.*

She slowly begins to undress. As she does so, her body is revealed to be covered in tiny cuts, scabs and bruises. Covered. She turns round so they all can see her. They watch. She puts the red shoes on. The men watch. She stands before them. They watch. She closes her eyes tight.

PINK. Zig-a-zig-ah.

Beat.

Zig-a-zig-ah.

She opens her eyes. Sees them still there. She begins to cry.

MALE VOICES. No crying. Crying's for babies. No crying.

She stops.

Good girl.

Beat.

Good girl.

She stands before them. A long time. She gets down on her hands and knees.

Good girl.

PINK *puts her head on the floor and covers her ears.*

ROLLY *returns. She opens the door purposefully. She goes straight to the table and picks up both of the wraps of heroin, deliberately not looking at* PINK. *She goes back to the door as if to leave. A pause.* ROLLY *turns to look at her sister. Pause. She moves to* PINK *and puts one of the wraps of heroin into* PINK*'s hand.* PINK *clutches it, but doesn't move. She remains on all-fours, her head on the ground.* ROLLY *stares down at her. Pause.* ROLLY *gets down on the floor. She tenderly takes* PINK *in her arms. Pause.* ROLLY *reaches for a syringe, foil, etc.* ROLLY *begins to hum 'If I Only Had a Brain.' The* MEN *fade away.* ROLLY *begins to cook up.*

The End.

Other Titles in this Series

Mike Bartlett
BULL
KING CHARLES III

Jez Butterworth
JERUSALEM
JEZ BUTTERWORTH PLAYS: ONE
MOJO
THE NIGHT HERON
PARLOUR SONG
THE RIVER
THE WINTERLING

Caryl Churchill
BLUE HEART
CHURCHILL PLAYS: THREE
CHURCHILL PLAYS: FOUR
CHURCHILL: SHORTS
CLOUD NINE
DING DONG THE WICKED
A DREAM PLAY *after* Strindberg
DRUNK ENOUGH TO SAY
    I LOVE YOU?
FAR AWAY
HOTEL
ICECREAM
LIGHT SHINING IN
    BUCKINGHAMSHIRE
LOVE AND INFORMATION
MAD FOREST
A NUMBER
SEVEN JEWISH CHILDREN
THE SKRIKER
THIS IS A CHAIR
THYESTES *after* Seneca
TRAPS

Stella Feehily
BANG BANG BANG
DREAMS OF VIOLENCE
DUCK
O GO MY MAN
THIS MAY HURT A BIT

Vivienne Franzmann
MOGADISHU
THE WITNESS

debbie tucker green
BORN BAD
DIRTY BUTTERFLY
NUT
RANDOM
STONING MARY
TRADE & GENERATIONS
TRUTH AND RECONCILIATION

Nancy Harris
LOVE IN A GLASS JAR
NO ROMANCE
OUR NEW GIRL

Vicky Jones
THE ONE

Dawn King
CIPHERS
FOXFINDER

Lucy Kirkwood
BEAUTY AND THE BEAST
    with Katie Mitchell
BLOODY WIMMIN
CHIMERICA
HEDDA *after* Ibsen
IT FELT EMPTY WHEN THE
    HEART WENT AT FIRST BUT
    IT IS ALRIGHT NOW
NSFW
TINDERBOX

Conor McPherson
DUBLIN CAROL
McPHERSON PLAYS: ONE
McPHERSON PLAYS: TWO
McPHERSON PLAYS: THREE
THE NIGHT ALIVE
PORT AUTHORITY
THE SEAFARER
SHINING CITY
THE VEIL
THE WEIR

Chloë Moss
CHRISTMAS IS MILES AWAY
HOW LOVE IS SPELT
FATAL LIGHT
THE GATEKEEPER
THE WAY HOME
THIS WIDE NIGHT

Bruce Norris
CLYBOURNE PARK
THE LOW ROAD
THE PAIN AND THE ITCH
PURPLE HEART

Janice Okoh
EGUSI SOUP
THREE BIRDS

Evan Placey
GIRLS LIKE THAT
PRONOUN

Jack Thorne
2ND MAY 1997
BUNNY
LET THE RIGHT ONE IN
    after John Ajvide Lindqvist
MYDIDAE
STACY & FANNY AND FAGGOT
WHEN YOU CURE ME

Phoebe Waller-Bridge
FLEABAG

Enda Walsh
BEDBOUND
    & MISTERMAN
DELIRIUM
DISCO PIGS & SUCKING DUBLIN
ENDA WALSH PLAYS: ONE
MISTERMAN
THE NEW ELECTRIC BALLROOM
ONCE
PENELOPE
THE SMALL THINGS
THE WALWORTH FARCE

A Nick Hern Book

Pests first published in Great Britain in 2014 as a paperback original by Nick Hern Books Limited, The Glasshouse, 49a Goldhawk Road, London W12 8QP, in association with Clean Break

Pests copyright © 2014 Vivienne Franzmann

Vivienne Franzmann has asserted her right to be identified as the author of this work

Cover photograph: Dan Bass
Image design: knownbyassociation.co.uk

Designed and typeset by Nick Hern Books, London
Printed and bound in Great Britain by CPI Group (UK) Ltd

A CIP catalogue record for this book is available from the British Library

ISBN 978 1 84842 380 0